MODERATE DRINKING MADE EASY WORKBOOK

MODERATE
DRINKING
MADE EASY
WORKBOOK

*Drinker-Friendly Tips and Exercises to Control Drinking
and Reduce Alcohol Craving and Consumption*

Donna J. Cornett, M.A.

People Friendly Books
Santa Rosa, California, USA

Moderate Drinking Made Easy Workbook
Drinker-Friendly Tips and Exercises to Control Drinking
and Reduce Alcohol Craving and Consumption

People Friendly Books

For information address:

People Friendly Books
P.O. Box 5441
Santa Rosa, CA 95402 USA
www.drinklinkmoderation.com

ISBN: 978-0-9763720-7-3

Library of Congress Control Number: 2008941463

Printed in the United States of America

To everyone who pulled me through 2008,
especially Darla Ravella, Dixie Rohrman, Dee Rodriquez,
Shirley and Lester Cornett, Dale Cornett and everyone at the
Center for Spiritual Living in Santa Rosa, California.

Contents

Introduction i

Disclaimer iii

Chapter One: Do You Have a Drinking Problem? 1

Chapter Two: Moderate Drinking Tips Before You Drink.............. 7

Chapter Three: Moderate Drinking Tips While You Drink............. 87

Chapter Four: Moderate Drinking Tips After You Drink............. 155

Chapter Five: How Are You Doing?... 209

About the Author.. 211

About Drink/Link™ Moderate Drinking Programs and Products....... 213

Introduction

Are you worried about your drinking, but think your only options are abstinence and AA? Over the years, I've noticed almost anyone who drinks alcohol becomes concerned about it at one time or another. Whether you drink too much, you drink too fast, you have an alcohol habit, you make a fool of yourself in social situations or you turn to liquor to cope, it's no fun to think you might have a drinking problem. Instead of alcohol enhancing the quality of your life, it poisons it. And the problem could get worse - ruining your health and relationships, landing you in jail, costing you court fines and attorney fees and destroying your reputation, self-confidence and self-esteem - to the point where you have to quit drinking.

If you're one of the millions of drinkers who's worried about your drinking, but has put off doing anything about it because you don't think it's serious enough to stop altogether or you've been brainwashed into believing abstinence programs are the only solution to any drinking problem and you're turned off by meetings and the required belief in a higher power, this book is for you.

The Moderate Drinking Made Easy Workbook is not a program, but a research-based collection of sensible drinking tips and exercises designed to help you reduce your alcohol craving and consumption, modify your drinking habits and prevent alcoholism. You'll learn dozens of before you drink, while you drink and after your drink skills and strategies, not only to master the art of moderate drinking, but the moderate drinking mindset as well. You can pick and choose the easy tips and insightful exercises you think will work for you. And you're encouraged to be proactive, to deeply reflect on each skill and suggestion and to brainstorm solutions to obstacles standing between you and better drinking habits. The more effort you put into this workbook, the more successful you'll be at controlling your drinking!

The Moderate Drinking Made Easy Workbook is for drinkers still capable of unlearning destructive drinking patterns and learning healthy new ones. If you think you're an alcoholic or have a serious drinking problem, practicing the tips in this book probably won't work for you. That is, reduce your drinking and prevent alcoholism. And if you use the information here to convince yourself or others that you are making an earnest effort to improve your drinking behavior, but you don't practice the skills you learn, you're fooling yourself. This book is not an excuse to continue to drink heavily or inappropriately. The truth will catch up to you sooner or later and you'll pay the price.

Remember - cultivating physical, psychological, intellectual and spiritual balance is the antidote to alcohol craving and abuse.

Donna J. Cornett
Founder and Director
Drink/Link Moderate Drinking Programs and Products

Disclaimer

The tips, skills and exercises in this book are not recommended for the alcoholic, anyone who has a serious drinking problem, anyone who has a physical or psychological condition aggravated by alcohol use, anyone who suffers from serious health, psychological, social, legal, financial or job-related problems as a result of alcohol use, any woman who is pregnant or thinking of becoming pregnant, any minor or anyone who has successfully abstained. Results vary according to the individual.

Chapter One:

Do You Have a Drinking Problem?

Maybe you drink socially, without any problems, most of the time. But every once in a while you slip and make a fool of yourself. Or perhaps you're concerned about a growing drinking habit and graduating to alcoholism. Maybe you're suffering from alcohol-related problems - health, family, social, work, financial and/or legal issues - because you're drinking too much or you're drinking inappropriately. Or you feel alcohol and drinking have become too important to you. Whatever your situation, you're about to learn dozens of healthy drinking skills to master the art of moderate drinking and the moderate drinking mindset as well.

But before you get to work, you have to examine your current drinking habits and understand exactly what "moderate drinking," "alcohol abuse" and "alcoholism" are. Knowing how serious your drinking is, is the first step to fixing it!

What is Moderate Drinking?

Moderate drinking is light, appropriate drinking suited to the occasion. You have no problems associated with alcohol and you never put yourself or others at risk because of it. Moderate drinking is . . .

- Limiting yourself to one, two or three drinks a day.
- Pacing yourself to one drink per hour.
- Light drinking while enjoying the company of others.
- Light drinking to celebrate a special occasion.
- Drinking a little to unwind at the end of the day.
- Drinking as a secondary activity - not the focus of your day.
- Light drinking in appropriate places, like your home, a friend's house, a restaurant.

On the other hand, drinking too much and too often is not moderate drinking. You may develop problems and put yourself and others at risk because of alcohol. Moderate drinking is not . . .

- Drinking as much as you can.
- Drinking as fast as you can.
- Drinking alone most of the time.
- Drinking for no special reason.
- Drinking to cope with emotions.
- Drinking to deal with stress.
- Drinking as your primary activity.
- Drinking everywhere - at home, work, club, car, etc.
- Drinking over your daily drink limit.

What is Problem Drinking?

Anyone who drinks should know the symptoms of alcohol abuse or problem drinking. Generally speaking, if you are experiencing any problems - health, family, interpersonal, work, legal or financial - because of alcohol use, you're suffering from alcohol abuse and you're a problem drinker.

According to the American Psychiatric Association, a person suffering from alcohol abuse or problem drinking displays one or more of the following symptoms within a 12-month period:

- Failure to meet work, school or home obligations because of recurrent alcohol use.
- Placing yourself in physically dangerous situations, like drinking and driving, because of recurrent alcohol use.
- Legal and/or financial problems resulting from recurrent alcohol use.
- Continuing to drink despite having alcohol-related social or interpersonal problems.

If you are dealing with one or more of these symptoms, you're a problem drinker. But the good news is you may still be capable of modifying your drinking habits and returning to problem free drinking.

What is Alcoholism?

According to the American Psychiatric Association, a person suffering from alcoholism or alcohol dependence displays three or more of the following symptoms within a 12-month period:

- Lowered tolerance to alcohol - the need to drink more and more alcohol to get high.
- Drinking more alcohol or over a longer period of time than you intend.
- Experiencing physical withdrawal symptoms, like stomach upset, headache, sweating, rapid pulse rate, tremors, insomnia or anxiety, if you reduce or stop drinking.

- A strong desire or attempting and failing at reducing or controlling your drinking.
- Spending too much time obtaining alcohol, drinking alcohol or recovering from the effects of alcohol - having a hangover.
- Limiting recreational, social or occupational activities because of alcohol.
- Continued drinking despite ongoing physical or psychological problems caused by or aggravated by alcohol use.

If you are experiencing three or more of these symptoms, you are an alcoholic and trying to control drinking would be difficult, if not impossible. You have a serious drinking problem and need to stop.

Get the Most Out Of Moderate Drinking Made Easy

This book is divided into several sections - before you drink, while you drink and after you drink tips and exercises - and you can use it several different ways. You can pick and choose the tips and skills you think will work for you. Or you can read and reflect on one tip from each section every day. Or you can practice a couple of suggestions a day from one section, completing that section before you move on to the next.

Be proactive and give a lot of thought to each tip and exercise. Practice each suggestion at least two times to see if it helps you drink less. Actually applying them to your drinking behavior and incorporating them into your lifestyle will be the key to your success. When you've completed the book, you will have developed a moderate drinking mindset and learned a large repertoire of safe drinking habits you can enjoy for the rest of your life.

Keep practicing the tips that work for you! That is, help you to reduce your alcohol craving and consumption and eliminate the problem drinking habits you're concerned about. Practice makes perfect. Perfect moderate drinking that is.

And stick with it! If you slip, get right back on track, instead of wallowing in guilt and shame. Leave the past behind, live in the present and refocus on your sensible drinking goal. There will be ups and downs on your moderate drinking journey, but that's normal.

What are you waiting for? It's time to make the switch to moderate drinking.

Chapter Two:

Moderate Drinking Tips Before You Drink

Henry David Thoreau said, "Things do not change; we change. " You're the driving force behind new, improved drinking behavior and don't forget it. And the tips and exercises in this chapter - change skills and strategies before you even take a sip of alcohol - are designed to get you excited about cutting down and thinking about how you'll handle yourself when you do drink.

ARE YOU READY FOR AN ALCOHOL ATTITUDE ADJUSTMENT?

C hanging the way you think about alcohol is the first step to changing your drinking behavior. And that means you'll have to make an alcohol attitude adjustment - constantly reminding yourself of how unimportant liquor is in the big picture of your life.

Every time your thoughts turn to booze - like obsessing about your first drink of the day - stop yourself and get back to the business of living. Put that cocktail in the back of your mind where it belongs and remind yourself a few drinks merely complement your wonderful, healthy life - they aren't your life. Then focus on family, friends, work, play, fun - people and activities that should be the center of your attention. They're so much more important than just another beer. That's how you'll start thinking and acting like a moderate drinker.

When do you start thinking about your first drink of the day? What will you say to yourself - keeping your alcohol attitude adjustment in mind - when craving strikes? Record your thoughts.

Moderate Drinking Made Easy Workbook

BE HONEST WITH YOURSELF

It's truth-telling time. Like being honest with yourself about how much you really drink. If you can't own up to how much you're really drinking, maybe you're not ready to switch to moderate drinking.

The truth will set you free. So when you're straight with yourself about your actual alcohol consumption, you'll be closer to making a positive change. FYI - one drink is considered five ounces of wine, twelve ounces of beer or one and a half ounces of hard liquor.

How much do you really drink everyday, every week? Think hard. Then record your current daily and weekly drink totals.

Notes

_____

_____

_____

_____

_____

_____

_____

_____

_____

_____

_____

_____

_____

_____

_____

_____

_____

EMBRACE YOUR DRINKING PROBLEM

That may sound funny, but it's no joke. Once you admit the problems alcohol has caused you and your loved ones, you'll be ready to make a brand new sensible drinking start.

How many hangovers have you had within the last week, the last month? Any health concerns associated with too much booze? Is alcohol getting in the way of your relationships with your spouse, family, friends, co-workers? Has anyone ever lectured you about your drinking problem? Are you missing work or punching in late because you're partying too much the night before? Have you been ticketed or arrested for drunk driving, driving under the influence or public drunkenness? Any money problems because of expensive alcohol-related legal fees or fines?

Get it off your chest and you'll be pointed in the right direction. When you're faltering or feeling challenged in the weeks ahead, you might refer to these problems to keep you on the straight and narrow.

List all of the negative ways liquor has impacted your life. And your loved one's lives.

FORGIVE YOURSELF
AND MOVE FORWARD

Give up the shame and guilt you're carrying from your old drinking ways. Feeling bad about yourself can stop you from changing before you even start - eating away at your self-confidence and self-esteem so you think you're incapable of being better.

It's time to forgive yourself, let go of the shame, guilt and embarrassment you feel over your problem drinking past and move forward. If you feel good about yourself, your chances of becoming a moderate drinker forever will improve significantly.

Yes, forgive yourself, but don't forget your antics when you were under the influence. Remembering how wild and crazy you were when you overdrank will motivate you to change.

Write about specific events in your past fueled by alcohol. Then, move on with a positive "can do" attitude.

Notes

_____

_____

_____

_____

_____

_____

_____

_____

_____

_____

_____

_____

_____

_____

_____

_____

_____

_____

_____

_____

MAKE A FIRM COMMITMENT

Before you can achieve anything, including moderate drinking, you must make a firm commitment to it. That means sticking with it through thick and thin. Even when the going gets tough.

Remind yourself of your commitment every day - especially if it's a drinking day or you're tempted to fall back into your old problem drinking pattern.

Record your moderate drinking commitment. Describe how switching to sensible drinking will change the course of your life, how you'll get right back on track if you stray and how you'll follow through with healthy drinking skills and strategies - even when you don't want to. You're a committed moderate drinker!

Moderate Drinking Made Easy Workbook

HUG CHANGE

Yes, you'll have to put your arms around change to make it happen. And you'll have to embrace major changes in your life to become a sensible drinker long-term.

Change can be a little scary at first. Feelings of anxiety, uneasiness and uncertainty often accompany it. Any departure from the status quo - like making your health, family and friends your priority, instead of booze - is bound to feel a little strange in the beginning. That's par for the course.

But instead of fighting those feelings, remind yourself they go with the territory. Be prepared to feel a little uncomfortable when modifying your drinking habits and attitudes. But hang in there. Keep in mind that practicing your healthy new drinking behaviors for just a couple of weeks will lessen your change anxiety and moderate drinking will get easier and easier. A change for the better!

Write about the feelings you think you'll experience when changing your drinking pattern.

Notes

_____

_____

_____

_____

_____

_____

_____

_____

_____

_____

_____

_____

_____

_____

_____

_____

_____

_____

HELLO MOTIVATION!

How badly do you want to change your drinking ways? If you want it so bad it hurts, you might have the right stuff - the motivation - to succeed. Strong motivation is the driving force behind any behavior change and increases your chances of safe drinking success.

How can you get fired up about improving your drinking habits? Everyday, especially before a drinking party, think about the pros of moderate drinking and the cons of problem drinking. It will intensify your motivation so you'll actually follow through with the healthy new drinking skills you're learning.

Rate your motivation on a scale from one to ten, with one being least motivated and ten being highly motivated. If you're a five or less, reaching your moderate drinking goal might be tough. You're just not that motivated. If you're a six or more, your chances of improving your drinking habits increase. How motivated are you? Record your answer.

Moderate Drinking Made Easy Workbook

A HEALTHY LIFESTYLE IS
THE ANTIDOTE TO ALCOHOL ABUSE

The happier and healthier you are, the less you'll turn to alcohol to feel better. So if you're not eating three square meals a day, if you're not getting enough rest or exercise or if you're not having enough good, clean fun, be careful. You're setting yourself up for problem drinking.

What is a healthy lifestyle? One where you eat three nutritious meals a day with lots of fruits, vegetables, whole grains and protein. No high-calorie or fatty junk food allowed. You get plenty of exercise - at least thirty minutes a day, three or four times a week. You get at least seven hours of sleep every night. You get out and party with people you like. And you feel good about yourself and the direction of your life. Live a wholesome lifestyle and reduced alcohol craving and consumption will come naturally.

Write down the lifestyle elements you need to improve, then follow through!

Notes

_____

_____

_____

_____

_____

_____

_____

_____

_____

_____

_____

_____

_____

_____

_____

_____

_____

START THINKING OUTSIDE
OF THE BOTTLE . . .

How long has it been since you enjoyed some free time without liquor? Since most of us are busy most of the time - consumed with work, family and getting ahead - thinking up activities you really enjoy that don't involve alcohol can be a real challenge. Now's the time to give some serious thought to making good times happen without booze, instead of the other way around.

What's your idea of fun? Rafting? Picnicking? Skiing? Bowling? Dancing? Miniature golfing? Vacationing? Camping? Cooking? Going to a soccer, basketball, football or baseball game? Taking a drive in the country? Antiquing? Catching a matinee? Painting a picture? Playing softball? Hiking in the woods? Going to the beach? Making love?

List five of your favorite alcohol-free activities. Then fit them into your schedule - instead of wasting your time drinking. Start thinking outside of the bottle and your stress level will go down along with your drinking.

WHAT IS THE
MODERATE DRINKING FORMULA?

E qual parts of commitment, motivation and sensible drinking actions, that's what it is. Pledging to improve your drinking habits, no matter what, is one element of the formula. Psyching yourself up to practice the healthy tips and skills you learn is the second element. And translating your sensible drinking thoughts into actions is the third element. It's that simple.

Write "Commitment, motivation and sensible drinking actions equal moderate drinking" ten times.

Notes

_____

_____

_____

_____

_____

_____

_____

_____

_____

_____

_____

_____

_____

_____

_____

_____

_____

YOU CONTROL YOUR
DRINKING AND YOUR LIFE

Y ou write your own story. How you conduct yourself and what you accomplish is up to you. That goes for your drinking too. Don't blame your abuse of alcohol on a disease, bad genes or a rotten childhood. You're the one who lifts the glass to your lips and you're the one who can put it down.

You're in charge - whether you like it or not. Isn't it empowering to know you determine the direction of your life and can change for the better if you really want to?

When was the last time you took charge and made a positive difference in your life? Write about it and how you felt, then transfer those empowering feelings to controlling your drinking.

CHOICES

Life is really just a series of choices. So is moderate drinking. Will I stick to my drink limit or won't I? Will I pace my drinking or won't I? Will I eat while I drink or won't I? Will I alternate with non-alcoholic beverages or won't I? Will I focus on family, friends, work, play or booze?

Choose moderate drinking and choose a healthy, happy life. Choose alcohol abuse and choose a life plagued with health, family, social, work, legal and financial problems. The choice is clear.

Record the moderate drinking choices you'll make in the next week. Then follow through with them!

WHAT'S YOUR DOMINANT DRINKING STYLE?

Are you a binge drinker? A habitual drinker? A stress drinker? A mood or emotional drinker? Or a combination of two, three or all four of them?

If you're a binge drinker, you drink until you're drunk. Most every time you drink, you go all out, get wasted, blackout and/or pass out. Or all three.

If you're a habitual drinker, you drink at about the same time and have the same number of drinks most every day. It's a rut you've gotten into that excludes any other activity at that time.

If you're a stress drinker, you use liquor to relieve the mental and physical tension of the day. You drink too much on a regular basis and rely on booze as your only stress-reducing activity.

If you're a mood or emotional drinker, you use alcohol to cope with good or bad feelings. Your thoughts turn to liquor to enhance good feelings or numb bad ones.

What drinking styles can you identify with? Write about them.

WHAT'S YOUR DRINKING HISTORY?

Did your parents drink? Never, occasionally, regularly? Sensibly or recklessly? Did either one ever abuse alcohol? How about your high school and college friends? Did they take their time or binge? Did any of them develop a drinking problem?

What did you learn about alcohol and drinking from your family and friends? How have they affected your attitudes and behavior around liquor? Take a look back. Maybe you can see how and why you developed your current drinking habits and mindset.

If you were taught to be a problem drinker, break with the past and cast off the alcohol abuse patterns you grew up with. You're an independent adult now and capable of replacing those old behaviors with healthy ones.

Describe drinking habits and attitudes you picked up from others and how they continue to affect you today.

Notes

_____

_____

_____

_____

_____

_____

_____

_____

_____

_____

_____

_____

_____

_____

_____

_____

_____

_____

_____

APPROPRIATE DRINKING IS THE ANSWER

Appropriate drinking is drinking suited to the occasion. Maybe it's a cocktail with appetizers before dinner, maybe one with dinner. Perhaps it's a martini or two when you're socializing with friends. Or a glass of champagne to celebrate a special occasion. Food, friends and good times are appropriate drinking settings. And it's only appropriate if you don't drink too much or too fast.

Reflect on the concept of appropriate drinking. Now, every time you take a sip of alcohol ask yourself, "Is this appropriate drinking?". In fact, make it a part of your drinking routine. It will make you more aware of how much you're drinking and you'll drink less naturally.

Think about your drinking occasions over the last month. Which ones were appropriate? What made them appropriate? Describe them.

INAPPROPRIATE DRINKING IS NOT THE ANSWER

Drinking too much, too fast or for no good reason is inappropriate drinking. It doesn't involve healthy eating, wholesome relationships or happy times. It can be mindless drinking because you're lonely or bored. Or it can be reflexive drinking because you're angry, depressed, stressed, anxious or frustrated.

How many inappropriate drinking occasions have you had over the last month? What made them inappropriate? Describe them.

Notes

_____

_____

_____

_____

_____

_____

_____

_____

_____

_____

_____

_____

_____

_____

_____

_____

_____

_____

_____

_____

WHAT'S YOUR PAYOFF FOR APPROPRIATE DRINKING?

Expect positive health, social, psychological and financial payoffs for sticking to moderate drinking long-term. You'll feel better in the morning - well-rested and energetic. In fact, you'll feel healthier in general. You'll get along better with mate, family, friends and colleagues when liquor doesn't get in the way. Alcohol-related work, financial and legal problems will disappear. You'll feel good about yourself - more self-confidence and greater self-esteem - because you're controlling your drinking and not getting drunk. And you'll enjoy a peace of mind you haven't felt in years when booze is no longer a monkey on your back.

No more alcohol-induced fits, blackouts or hangovers, no more driving under the influence and no more damage to your reputation because of too much liquor. Just think of all you'll miss when you switch to moderate drinking!

How much better will your life be - physically, psychologically, socially and financially - when you switch to healthier drinking habits? List your payoffs.

Moderate Drinking Made Easy Workbook

WHAT DOES YOUR
PAYOFF PEP TALK SOUND LIKE?

You can finally fulfill your fantasy of becoming a recording artist. Now that you've given a lot of thought to how moderate drinking will improve the quality of your life, record your payoffs on a CD or audio cassette.

This is your payoff pep talk. Listen to it every day and before every drinking event, especially if you're facing a challenge. It will motivate you to practice the sensible drinking skills and strategies you're learning. Write your payoff pep talk script, then record it

Notes

_____

_____

_____

_____

_____

_____

_____

_____

_____

_____

_____

_____

_____

_____

_____

_____

RAISE YOUR DRINKING AWARENESS AND LOWER YOUR ALCOHOL CONSUMPTION

After years of drinking, most of us don't have a clue about how much we really drink. We don't pay attention to how fast we're guzzling and we drink until we get high or drunk. We're totally unaware.

Change is in the wind. It's time to raise your drinking awareness - to become aware of how much and how fast you actually drink. Why? Because research shows the more sensitive you are to how much and how fast you drink, the less you'll drink - automatically. Sweet!

Recognizing when the desire to drink strikes, counting your drinks, timing your drinks, tuning in to self-talk that encourages you to drink and keeping a drinking diary will all raise your drinking awareness and lower your alcohol consumption - effortlessly.

Describe how you'll raise your drinking awareness in the coming weeks.

Moderate Drinking Made Easy Workbook

RAISE YOUR DRINKING
TRIGGER AWARENESS TOO

What drives you to drink? Internal cues or external cues? Or a combination of both? External cues are the easiest to spot - like the time of day you drink, your drinking companions, places where you drink or the sight and smell of alcohol.

Internal cues, physiological and psychological states - like hunger, fatigue, anxiety, stress, anger, frustration, boredom, loneliness or depression - may also trip your desire to drink. Give your internal drinking cues serious thought because they're more difficult to identify than external ones.

Once you become familiar with the cues triggering your drinking desire, start dealing with them appropriately and you'll drink less. Stop hanging out at your old watering hole with your barfly buddies. Practice stress management techniques to loosen up. Eat if you're hungry. Enroll in a dance class to get busy. Talk to a professional counselor about your feelings instead of pouring yourself a tall one.

What drives you to drink? Record your internal and external drinking cues and how you'll manage with them without a cocktail.

Notes

_____

_____

_____

_____

_____

_____

_____

_____

_____

_____

_____

_____

_____

_____

_____

_____

_____

_____

_____

_____

START A DRINKING DIARY - AND CUT DOWN EFFORTLESSLY

The more you raise your drinking awareness, the less you'll drink. And keeping a drinking diary will do just that. It will sensitize you to how much and how fast you're drinking and reduce your alcohol consumption naturally.

Start a drinking diary today. From now on, every time you drink, record how many drinks you have, how long you drink, the date, day, time, place, companions, circumstances, physiological cues you may be experiencing, like hunger, thirst or fatigue, and psychological cues you may be experiencing, like boredom, stress, loneliness, frustration, anger, depression or anxiety. Remember - one and a half ounces of spirits, five ounces of wine and twelve ounces of beer are each considered one drink. No cheating!

Another advantage to keeping a drinking diary? Over time, you'll get smarter about the internal and external cues that trigger your problem drinking and, hopefully, you'll start handling them appropriately so they no longer lead to overdrinking.

Moderate Drinking Made Easy Workbook

Get busy and jot down a sample page of your drinking diary. Include drink total, drinking time, date, day, time, place, companions, circumstances and physiological and psychological cue columns. Then record your sample page in a blank notebook and list every drinking occasion from now on.

Notes

_____

_____

_____

_____

_____

_____

_____

_____

_____

_____

_____

_____

_____

_____

_____

_____

_____

_____

SET A REALISTIC DAILY DRINK LIMIT

How often have you walked into a drinking party cold - with no idea of how much or how long you'll drink - and before you know it, the alcohol takes over and you've had too much.

It's time for you to set your daily drink limit. Maybe one, two or three cocktails on some days, maybe none on others. Of course, a lot depends on you - your weight, gender and personal preference. The smaller you are, the less alcohol you need to get high, so limit yourself to one or two. And women metabolize alcohol slower than men, so ladies, keep your drink limit low. FYI - three drinks a day is plenty and should be the maximum daily drink limit for anyone.

It's also probably a good idea to give yourself a drink range - like one to two drinks or two to three drinks - depending on the circumstances. Boxing yourself into a specific number may cause you to rebel, drink too much and revert back to your old problem-drinking ways. Thinking in range terms doesn't box you in and

Moderate Drinking Made Easy Workbook

gives you some wiggle room so you don't rebel and overdrink

Whether you have one, two or the max of three drinks on a given day may depend on the situation. If you've had a rough day, you're tired and get home late, making sure you have your three drinks would be silly. No alcohol might be best. If, however, you're out with friends and have a designated driver, perhaps three drinks over three or four hours with dinner, dessert and coffee would do. You need to look at each drinking event in advance and determine how much liquor, if any, is appropriate.

Don't feel obligated to have your limit every time you drink. That kind of thinking keeps you focused on booze and doesn't cultivate your alcohol attitude adjustment. Considering your ultimate goal is to make wise decisions on your own as to when, how long and how much you'll drink, without having to count your drinks, maxing out every time you drink defeats that purpose and doesn't nurture wise drinking decisions.

Notes

_____

_____

_____

_____

_____

_____

_____

_____

_____

_____

_____

_____

_____

_____

_____

_____

_____

_____

Notes

_____

_____

_____

_____

_____

_____

_____

_____

_____

_____

_____

_____

_____

_____

_____

_____

A word of caution if you set too ambitious of a daily drink limit in the beginning - say one or two drinks per day and two or three abstinent days per week - when you're used to drinking everyday and having three or more. You're setting yourself up for failure. Instead, take your time and get your arms around small changes first. For example, start with one abstinent day per week and two to three glasses with food on drinking days. Small successes will increase your self-confidence and self-control and lead to bigger successes down the road. Eventually, you can add more abstinent days and reduce your alcohol consumption even more. Take it slow and be patient with yourself.

Now, set your daily drink limit range and record it.

Moderate Drinking Made Easy Workbook

SET A REALISTIC WEEKLY DRINK LIMIT TOO

Setting and sticking to a weekly drink limit is also an important leg of your moderate drinking journey. If you allow yourself five drinking days a week and have two to three drinks per day, your weekly drink range will be ten to fifteen drinks. Again, don't feel obligated to have your fifteen drink max every week. Some weeks, when you have lots going on, you probably shouldn't max out. You're too busy to drink. On the other hand, if you're attending several social functions during the week, you might reach your high number. A lot depends on what comes up.

Always keep your daily and weekly drink limits in the back of your mind, then decide in advance how many drinks would be appropriate for every future drinking occasion. Make a real effort to stick to your limit and eventually you'll no longer need to count your drinks. There is light at the end of the tunnel!

Jot down your weekly drink limit range. Then record your weekly drink total for every week from now on. Is your alcohol consumption going down?

Notes

_____
_____
_____
_____
_____
_____
_____
_____
_____
_____
_____
_____
_____
_____
_____
_____
_____
_____
_____
_____
_____

WHAT'S YOUR POINT OF NO RETURN?

I t's when you've had so many drinks you're not thinking straight, your judgment is impaired and you're unable to make the right decision as to when to slow down or stop drinking.

For most people, the point of no return is at a .06 Blood Alcohol Concentration (BAC) level. At this level, you're more than relaxed, you're tipsy, and you're liable to forget all about your drink limit and your moderate drinking commitment. It's dangerous. But if you stay under a .06 BAC level, you can still enjoy yourself and you know when to stop. You're still in control and can stick to your limit.

How many drinks over one, two and three hours puts you at or above a .06 BAC level? Refer to the Blood Alcohol Concentration level charts provided by the Department of Motor Vehicles in your state. Record these numbers, then memorize them so you never go overboard again.

WHAT DOES YOUR DRINKING THINKING SOUND LIKE?

Drinking thinking is thinking that encourages you to drink too much, too fast and too often. It's thinking that convinces you the more alcohol you drink, the better you'll feel. It's thinking that fools you into believing if you don't keep up with hard drinking pals, you're not one of the guys. It's thinking that gives you permission to start or continue drinking, even though it's not appropriate to do so.

"It's five - happy hour - time for a drink." "I always have one for the road." "A couple of drinks before the party will loosen me up." "Booze will chase away my bad mood." "It's Friday night - of course I'm going out drinking!" "What's dinner without a scotch before, a couple of glasses of wine with my meal and a nightcap after?" "I always down a six-pack when I'm watching a football game." "If I feel this good after three martinis, I'll feel even better with a fourth." "I have nothing better to do, so I'll just sit and drink." Prime examples of dangerous drinking thinking.

Notes

_____

_____

_____

_____

_____

_____

_____

_____

_____

_____

_____

_____

_____

_____

_____

_____

_____

_____

There are thousands of crazy reasons to rationalize heavy drinking. The time of the day excuse, the one for the road excuse, the social lubricant excuse, the elevate my mood excuse, the sports event excuse, the dinner excuse and the boredom excuse are just a few. Most drinking thinking excuses are not logical, but lead to problem drinking anyway.

But you do have a choice: believe this destructive self-talk, act on it and overdrink or don't believe it, don't act on it and stay within your drink limit. If you don't fall for it, you're well on your way to thinking and acting like a moderate drinker naturally.

What does your drinking thinking sound like? Describe it. Then dissect the logic behind it and you'll be less susceptible to it.

POSITIVE SELF-TALK
DEFEATS DRINKING THINKING

The next time you're wrestling with dangerous drinking thinking, just stop! Stop the destructive inner conversation going on inside of your head encouraging you to drink heavily. Then switch to positive self-talk that will keep you on track.

Positive self-talk, like telling yourself how good you'll feel in the morning - physically and mentally - when you don't exceed your limit. Confident your reputation and relationships will still be in tact when you keep your cool and stop drinking. Feeling pleased that you're drinking like a responsible adult - not a bingeing adolescent. And knowing you'll enjoy a happier, healthier life free from alcohol abuse. There are so many logical reasons for you to stick to your drink limits!

What does your positive self-talk sound like when you're feeling challenged? Write it down and refer to it the next time you're tempted to go overboard.

Notes

_____

_____

_____

_____

_____

_____

_____

_____

_____

_____

_____

_____

_____

_____

_____

_____

_____

_____

_____

PRE-PLANNING YOUR DRINKING BEHAVIOR IS A MUST

Knowing exactly how you'll behave around alcohol before you even start drinking is key to reducing your alcohol consumption. You plan for work, you plan for school, you plan your social life and you plan your vacation. Why not plan for drinking too? From now on, whether you're home alone, eating out or partying with friends, you're devising and following through with a drinking plan of action.

Your basic plan should include setting a drink limit and time limit for every drinking occasion. Then brainstorm specific strategies and techniques to help you stay within those limits, like pacing yourself and allowing at least forty minutes for each drink, taking a timeout between drinks, eating before and during drinking, alternating with non-alcoholic drinks, distracting yourself with people, conversation and activities and paying close attention to your drinking etiquette - sipping, not gulping, and putting your drink down between sips.

Say you're invited to a dinner party at an old friend's house and you

Moderate Drinking Made Easy Workbook

know there will be lots of booze. In the past, you overdrank at these parties. You didn't have a plan. But times have changed and you've developed a drinking plan for this event. You'll have no more than two to three drinks - your daily limit range - for the night. That's a given. You've decided three drinking hours is more than enough time to imbibe. You'll start the evening with appetizers and a soft drink. When you do have that first cocktail, you'll nurse it. You'll watch the clock and take a ten or twenty minute timeout between drinks too. No need to rush your good time. You'll have seltzer water with a twist to slow down between drinks. You'll concentrate on socializing, not drinking. And you'll watch your drinking manners. No guzzling allowed. If you're tempted to have another drink after dinner, have coffee and dessert or just leave - out of sight, out of mind. You've had your fun and you'll feel great in the morning. Not like in times past.

Remember the good old days when you didn't have a plan, you drank mindlessly and you got drunk? They

Notes

weren't so good after all. But now, if you pre-plan and follow through, you'll be thinking and acting like a sensible drinker in no time.

What drinking occasions are coming up for you in the next two weeks? Write down a plan for each one - whether you're home alone or out partying. Then stick to it!

GET TO KNOW YOUR MOMENT OF TRUTH

Ahhh . . . the moment of truth. It arrives sooner or later. It's that moment when you're trying to decide if you should start drinking or stop drinking.

"It's too early in the day for a glass of wine, but I want one anyway." "I'd really enjoy another cocktail after lunch, even though I shouldn't." "I'd like a couple of martinis to loosen up before this party, even though it's not in my drinking plan." "I've had my drink limit, but everyone else is having more so I might as well." Sound familiar? Moments of truth most of us have experienced.

Sensitize yourself to the inner conversation going on inside of your head when you're facing your moment of truth. Then say no to the self-talk persuading you to start drinking inappropriately or continue drinking even though you've had your limit and say yes to your moderate drinking commitment. Remind yourself of your commitment and you'll conquer your moment of truth.

When was the last time you faced your moment of truth? What did your inner conversation sound like? Describe it.

Notes

_____

_____

_____

_____

_____

_____

_____

_____

_____

_____

_____

_____

_____

_____

_____

_____

_____

_____

_____

_____

Moderate Drinking Made Easy Workbook

WHAT'S YOUR MOMENT OF TRUTH PLAN?

Hopefully, you'll know when you're facing your moment of truth. If you don't recognize it at first, you'll know you're confronting it when you've finished the last drink of your daily drink limit and you still want more.

If you're having trouble saying no to more booze and saying yes to your moderate drinking commitment, when you're facing your moment of truth, develop a simple plan. Switch to a non-alcoholic drink? Read the newspaper? Pet the dog? Go to bed? Brush your teeth? Have safe sex? Give yourself a payoff pep talk? Having a plan up your sleeve might turn the tide. Try it.

Now get busy and write down your moment of truth plan - what you'll do instead of starting to drink or continuing to drink. Then follow through with it when the time is right.

Moderate Drinking Made Easy Workbook

WHAT ARE YOU REACHING FOR WHEN YOU REACH FOR A DRINK?

friend? A party? A vacation? A shrink? A pain pill? Many people who drink too much are trying to fill a void in their life. True, a little liquor may make you feel more loved and less lonely. It may improve your mood and numb the pain. But long-term heavy use will lead to dependence and actually prevent you from finding real love, real companionship, real entertainment, real understanding and real relief. You're too busy drinking alcohol to do anything else - like satisfying your needs appropriately.

What voids are you trying to fill with that cocktail? List them.

Notes

_____

_____

_____

_____

_____

_____

_____

_____

_____

_____

_____

_____

_____

_____

_____

_____

_____

_____

_____

_____

DON'T FORGET
ALCOHOL-FREE DAYS!

Not drinking a couple of days a week is a great idea. It will get you out of your old drinking rut, put alcohol in perspective and fine tune your alcohol attitude adjustment.

If you're not use to abstaining, start small with just one alcohol-free day a week. Once you get over that hurdle and feel more confident, have two or three. Be patient with yourself and you should be able to work up to several alcohol-free days a week within a couple of months.

Here are some tips to stay away from booze. Try to schedule your non-drinking days when you're consumed with work, family and activities. Keeping busy, especially in the beginning, makes not drinking or not thinking about drinking a lot easier. For example, if you don't have a spare moment on Mondays because you're tending to work, chores, kids, commitments and exercise, where could you possibly fit in that glass of wine? No where.

Plan lots of distracting activities during your regular drinking time too. If happy hour starts after work as soon as you walk in the door, plan on fruit juice with sparkling water, have a snack, read the newspaper, watch a DVD, take a shower, knit a scarf, do a crossword puzzle, clean the kitchen or write about your feelings when you abstain. Get the idea? Having tons of stuff to do takes your mind off liquor and before you know it, you will have forgotten all about the cocktail.

Yes, you may feel a bit deprived and uncomfortable the first couple of days you don't drink. That's normal whenever you're changing a pattern of behavior. Just be prepared for those feelings and know your change anxiety will pass after just a couple of non-drinking days. On the plus side, your self-confidence and self-esteem will soar. You'll prove you can live without liquor. A big payoff!

Every week look ahead and decide which days you'll opt out of drinking. List the days you'll abstain in the next two weeks.

Notes
_____
_____
_____
_____
_____
_____
_____
_____
_____
_____
_____
_____
_____
_____
_____
_____
_____
_____

GO ON THE WAGON
FOR THIRTY DAYS

Taking a timeout from alcohol, before you actually commit to moderate drinking, might work for you in several different ways. First, you'll put a stop to your old drinking routine and start with a clean slate. And after a couple of alcohol-free weeks, you'll forget all about booze. Second, not drinking for a time will lower your tolerance to liquor, so when you do start up again a little will go a long way. You'll get that warm, fuzzy feeling with only one or two drinks - not four or five - like in the old days. Third, not drinking for a month will make you feel good about yourself and increase your feelings of self-confidence and self-control. And finally, after quitting for a while, moderating your alcohol consumption may be easier and a drink or two will seem like a treat.

What's the secret to going on the wagon? Keeping busy! Instead of sitting around moping because you're not drinking, write a list of all the things you'll do in its place. You'll be amazed at how much you get done.

What activities are you planning to fill your old drinking times? Jot them down.

Moderate Drinking Made Easy Workbook

REPLACE YOUR DRINKING HABIT WITH A HEALTHY ONE

Next time you start thinking about having an inappropriate cocktail, do a crossword puzzle. People who do crossword puzzles are less likely to suffer from memory loss and Alzheimer's in their old age. Or pour yourself some fruit or vegetable juice - loaded with vitamins and minerals - to strengthen your immune system. Or do twenty sit-ups to tone your abs. Or call a friend and have a good laugh. Or chill out with a relaxation CD. Or meditate and get in touch with your serene spiritual self. Do something healthy instead of drinking!

List all the healthy habits you'll replace that inappropriate cocktail with.

Notes

_____

_____

_____

_____

_____

_____

_____

_____

_____

_____

_____

_____

_____

_____

_____

_____

_____

_____

LIMIT YOUR HAPPY HOUR

Instead of starting at five, start at six. Instead of stopping at nine, stop at eight. Start drinking an hour later and stop drinking an hour earlier. You'd be surprised at how much you could cut down if you limited your drinking time. You'll still enjoy the relaxing, euphoric glow of a couple of glasses, but you won't get too high and lose control.

Reduce your happy hour, reduce your alcohol consumption. Record your old start and stop times and your new ones.

Moderate Drinking Made Easy Workbook

NO DRINKING BEFORE OR AFTER A DRINKING EVENT

This is a no-brainer. Unless you're the perfect moderate drinker, you've probably never questioned having a drink or two before or after a social drinking occasion. It loosens you up, makes you feel friendlier and puts you in a party mood. Unfortunately, those before and after drinks really add up. If you have one, two or three drinks at the drinking event, in addition to the one or two you have before and/or after it, you'll probably blow your drink limit and you might get drunk.

This is your last call for before and after drinks. Start questioning them and eliminating them. You can still have fun with a couple of cocktails at the event - without those before and after drinks - but you'll stay within your limit and you won't get drunk. And you'll feel so good the next morning - even after a party!

Write "I will not drink before or after a social drinking occasion" ten times.

Notes

_____

_____

_____

_____

_____

_____

_____

_____

_____

_____

_____

_____

_____

_____

_____

_____

_____

_____

_____

NO DRINKING
AFTER DINNER

So many of us have a drink or two before dinner, a drink or two with dinner and a drink or two after dinner. And before you know it, we've had four, five or six cocktails. More than our limit and enough for a hangover.

Drinkers who practice the "no drinking after dinner" rule swear by it. Planning ahead NOT to continue drinking after dinner is the secret. In the beginning, after eating, make sure you have plenty of snacks, non-alcoholic beverages and distracting activities on hand to fill the gap that alcohol use to fill. After a couple of weeks, you will have forgotten all about that nightcap that was so important to you. Who would've thought that modifying your drinking habits could be so easy?

Could it work for you? Record the snacks, non-alcoholic beverages and activities you'll have lined up for dessert, instead of another martini.

DEVISE AN END OF THE DRINKING DAY RITUAL

It might be a chocolate chip cookie or a hot fudge sundae. It might be a soak in the hot tub. Perhaps it's a cappuccino or a good book. Or a bubble bath. Or munching on popcorn and watching movies.

The next time you hit your drink limit and you know it's time to stop, reach for your end of the drinking day ritual instead of another cocktail. Pre-plan something special. No need to feel deprived when you're reducing your alcohol consumption. Then do it when the time comes!

What's your pleasure? Jot it down.

Notes

_____

_____

_____

_____

_____

_____

_____

_____

_____

_____

_____

_____

_____

_____

_____

_____

_____

_____

YOU MANAGE CRAVING, IT DOESN'T MANAGE YOU

Some experts think of alcohol craving as an emotion that will pass with time - disappearing in as little as ten or fifteen minutes. Others compare it to a wave in the ocean. Starting slowly, gaining in intensity, washing over you, then fading back into the sea.

When the desire to drink strikes, remind yourself you're bigger and stronger than any craving. And you manage it, it doesn't mange you!

When was the last time you experienced a strong alcohol craving? What did it feel like? Describe your feelings.

Moderate Drinking Made Easy Workbook

CRAVINGS ARE PREDICTABLE

T he clock strikes five and you're ready for a cocktail. You're fighting a fierce alcohol craving. Or you're home alone, bored, and can hardly wait to mix your first martini. Staring drinking desire right in the eye. Or you're angry and upset and want to drown your sorrows in a vodka tonic. Alcohol craving strikes again!

Your desire to drink is quite predictable and can be triggered by a number of internal and external variables. Maybe it's time of day. At five your work day ends and the party begins. Maybe it's boredom or loneliness. And alcohol becomes your best friend. Maybe it's an emotion or state of mind. And liquor becomes your therapist.

What variables trip your alcohol craving? List them.

Notes

_____

_____

_____

_____

_____

_____

_____

_____

_____

_____

_____

_____

_____

_____

_____

_____

_____

_____

_____

_____

_____

SIMPLE STRATEGIES TO MANAGE CRAVING

Here are some tips to manage the variables that trip your drinking desire. First, try to eliminate the cue. For example, stop associating with overdrinking pals that encourage problem drinking or have a snack if you think hunger might factor into your need to drink. Second, try to modify the cue, like limiting the time you spend at your old watering hole or having a beer instead of your favorite cocktail. Third, change the way you think about the cue, like telling yourself having a vodka tonic to cope with emotions is an inappropriate use of alcohol or having a glass of wine with lunch isn't really necessary.

What tips are you going to apply to your drinking cues? Describe your plans.

WAIT OUT YOUR CRAVING

What will you do the next time drinking desire strikes? The easiest thing to do is just wait it out. It will pass and when it does you'll know you can meet a craving head on and survive without giving in to it and drinking. Simply wait out your cravings and moderate drinking will follow.

What will you say to yourself the next time you're consumed with alcohol craving? Record it.

Notes

_____

_____

_____

_____

_____

_____

_____

_____

_____

_____

_____

_____

_____

_____

_____

_____

_____

_____

_____

BALANCE YOUR LIFE AND
ALCOHOL CRAVING VANISHES

M any alternative medical systems believe if you lead a wholesome, balanced life you can prevent and cure disease. Apply this same philosophy to alcohol craving and abuse. That is, if you paid more attention to balancing your life - equalizing the physical, psychological, intellectual and spiritual aspects of it - your desire to drink may fade and you'd reduce your alcohol intake naturally.

Objectively examine your life and lifestyle. What do you go overboard on? What do you neglect? Do you work too much or too little? Play too much or too little? Are you a couch potato or a fitness freak? A healthy eater or a junk food junkie? Are you obsessed with money or could you care less about it? Do you nurture your spiritual side or ignore it? Your life may be out of sync and it could lead to problem drinking.

List the aspects of your life that need a little more TLC or a little less enthusiasm.

EAT RIGHT AND
ALCOHOL CRAVING VANISHES

Research shows that eating a nutritious, well-balanced diet can chase away alcohol craving. Healthy meals and snacks stabilize your blood sugar levels and elevate your mood. As a result, you find it easier to say no to drinking desire and to stick to your drink limit.

Snacking on junk food all day, on the other hand, sets you up for craving and alcohol abuse. Greasy, sugary, high-calorie food may be convenient at the time, but it doesn't do a thing for your attitude. Your blood sugar levels and mood yoyo, making it more difficult to fight alcohol craving and problem drinking.

What's on your menu for today? What's on your menu for the week? Write them down. Stick to a healthier diet and see how good you feel and how little you drink . . .

Notes

_____

_____

_____

_____

_____

_____

_____

_____

_____

_____

_____

_____

_____

_____

_____

_____

_____

EXERCISE AND
ALCOHOL CRAVING VANISHES

Being active is also a great way to improve your mood and reduce your drinking desire. If you don't have a regular exercise program, take the stairs, instead of the elevator. Ride your bike to the market, instead of driving. Vacuum the house. Weed the garden. Healthy activity doesn't have to be confined to a gym.

You might also consider a vigorous exercise routine three or four times a week. Do something you like to do - swim, bike, lift weights, practice yoga, play tennis or golf. Whatever turns you on. You'll really get those endorphins going - decreasing tension and stress and increasing feelings of well-being. And the less stressed and more relaxed you are, the less you'll need that martini to settle down.

List physical activities you're planning for the coming week. Then fit them into your schedule and follow through!

Moderate Drinking Made Easy Workbook

GET YOUR REST AND ALCOHOL CRAVING VANISHES

Seventy percent of Americans are sleep deprived. Are you one of them? If you're not getting at least seven or eight hours of sleep every night, you are. And it's hard to resist an extra drink when you're exhausted.

This is your wake-up call. Get to bed earlier, sleep in later and do whatever it takes to get more rest. You'll feel better - physically and mentally. And you'll find it easier to say no to alcohol craving and more drinks.

What's your plan to squeeze in eight hours every night? Record it and stick with it.

Notes

_____

_____

_____

_____

_____

_____

_____

_____

_____

_____

_____

_____

_____

_____

_____

_____

_____

_____

SATISFY PHYSIOLOGICAL NEEDS AND ALCOHOL CRAVING VANISHES

You'd be surprised at how many people turn to alcohol to satisfy physiological needs - and they're not even aware of it. They drink because they're thirsty, hungry, tired, in pain or want a blast of energy. And alcohol works, but it's an inappropriate use of it.

Tune in to your body every time you feel the urge to drink. What is it telling you? Then eat if you're hungry, hydrate yourself with water or juice if you're thirsty, take a nap if you're tired or talk to your healthcare professional about pain management if you're hurting. It's easy to cut down when you listen to your body and stop confusing physiological needs with alcohol craving.

List how many times you want a cocktail to satisfy physical needs in the coming week.

FIX YOUR PROBLEMS AND ALCOHOL CRAVING VANISHES

Low self-esteem, anxiety, depression, frustration, stress and anger have all been shown to increase alcohol consumption. It makes sense if you can resolve the issues eating at you, the less interest you'll have in liquor.

Start by studying up on the problem. Knowledge is power so go to the library and read everything you can get your hands on about the subject. Next, brainstorm solutions to fix it. If you're having a hard time coming up with answers, consider professional help - psychological counseling or life coaching.

What's stepping on your good time? Write about it and possible solutions to resolve it. Then fix it.

Notes

TWENTY-FIVE DIFFERENT WAYS
TO BEAT ALCOHOL CRAVING

When you're tempted to start or continue drinking, even though you know you shouldn't, do something to take your mind off of that craving. Tidy up the house, play with the dog, clean out a drawer, wash the car, make brownies, meditate, have a cup of coffee, pray. Fix dinner, give yourself a manicure, read the paper, have a soft drink. Take a walk, call a friend, water the garden, go shopping, write in your journal, get busy with a craft, dance. Start writing your novel, go bowling, take a bath, brush your teeth, do the dishes, clean the garage. Whatever works so you can delay that first drink or successive drinks.

When you distract yourself with an activity, you'll forget all about that martini for at least ten or fifteen minutes, maybe longer. And, over time, putting off that craving will become the norm.

Record twenty-five distracting activities to take your mind off of alcohol craving and follow through with them when the time comes!

COULD DARK CHOCOLATE SATISFY ALCOHOL CRAVING?

Two reasons why people drink alcohol is to improve their mood and increase their energy. You might get the same effects from dark chocolate. It could elevate your mood, give you the boost you're looking for and as a result, step on your alcohol craving.

Lucky you! It's as good as it gets when dark chocolate can reduce your drinking desire. Besides, the dark stuff is rich in antioxidants and is thought to improve cardiovascular health. Bye bye booze, hello chocolate!

In addition to chocolate, what other favorite foods might improve your attitude and reduce your alcohol craving? Jot them down.

Notes

_____

_____

_____

_____

_____

_____

_____

_____

_____

_____

_____

_____

_____

_____

_____

_____

_____

_____

_____

DON'T DRINK, VISUALIZE

Before you start drinking, take ten minutes. Close your eyes and practice deep breathing. First, exhale all of the stale air out of your lungs. Then take a deep breath and hold it for five seconds. Slowly exhale and while you're exhaling mentally say to yourself "relax." Take another deep breath and hold it for five seconds. Again, slowly exhale and say "relax" to yourself. Concentrate on deep breathing for several minutes. Each time you exhale, repeat "relax" to yourself and let go of all your worries.

Then visualize yourself in the woods or at the beach or in a beautiful garden. Imagine the still dampness of the forest and smell the tree perfume. Or feel the sun beating down on you, a cool breeze on your face and sand between your toes at the beach. Or relax to the water sounds of a fountain in a lovely garden. You feel far removed from the ups and downs of everyday life. You don't have a care in the world and feel completely at peace. Continue to visualize your serene setting for at least five minutes or until you feel totally relaxed.

Moderate Drinking Made Easy Workbook

Enjoy your quiet time. It may also quiet your need to drink. Next happy hour, instead of automatically pouring that cocktail, settle yourself down with deep breathing and visualization. Get in touch with your peaceful side, not that martini.

Describe your perfect setting. Then go there when you're thinking about drinking.

Notes

_____
_____
_____
_____
_____
_____
_____
_____
_____
_____
_____
_____
_____
_____
_____
_____
_____
_____

TRANSCEND YOUR DESIRE TO DRINK WITH A GARDEN MEDITATION

Planting flowers, pinching herbs, pruning bushes and pulling weeds will take your mind off of liquor in no time. Your garden will appreciate it too. You'll get so wrapped up in what you're doing, you'll forget all about that glass of wine.

Seriously, garden meditation - getting lost in the activity of gardening - is an excellent method to delay the first or successive drinks of the day. It's a wonderful way to avoid mindless drinking when you're alone or bored and a great "end of the drinking day" ritual.

You don't have to have a good-sized garden to derive the benefits of garden meditation. A small patio with tropical flowers, a room full of indoor plants, a window herb garden or a little vegetable patch will do. Next time your cocktail hour calls, get busy and nurture something other than your drinking habit.

What plants need your undivided attention? What plants will you pick up on your next trip to the nursery? Write about what needs to be done in your garden.

Moderate Drinking Made Easy Workbook

OR PERHAPS MUSIC MEDITATION IS MORE TO YOUR LIKING

Forget about that vodka tonic. Get rid of the beer. Put down that glass of wine. Instead, pop in your favorite CD and get lost in the music, rather than focusing on your alcohol craving and drinking.

If you use liquor to get in touch with your spiritual self - and many people do - you may be able to achieve that soulful high with music. Perhaps classical music will settle you down. Or rock 'n roll will charge you up. Or blues. Or jazz. Or country. What are your favorites? Get into the music, not the bourbon.

Music meditation works if you plan ahead. Make sure your selections are all lined up and ready to go before you even start thinking about drinking.

What music will you listen to in place of that cocktail? List your lineup.

Notes

_____

_____

_____

_____

_____

_____

_____

_____

_____

_____

_____

_____

_____

_____

_____

_____

_____

_____

SIMPLIFY, SIMPLIFY, SIMPLIFY

Is your life too complicated? Are you stretched to the limit with kids, career and housework? Do you have a "to do" list a mile long? Do you work fifty or sixty hours a week? Do you think being a good parent means running your kids from dance lessons to soccer games to tennis lessons to sleepovers to school projects to swimming lessons? Are you always on the run and frazzled by the end of the day? If you answer yes to any of these questions, you're probably doing too much.

It's difficult, if not impossible, to stick to moderate drinking plans when you're constantly on the go because behavior change requires energy. Energy to follow through with pre-planned sensible drinking skills and strategies. So if you're worn out most of the time, you don't have the energy it takes to modify your drinking habits and attitudes.

What activities you can eliminate or cut down on? How about prioritizing your chores and activities so you get the most important ones done first? Or planning some quiet time with absolutely nothing to do? Think about it. The simple life will recharge your batteries and generate the energy you need to switch to moderate drinking.

Slow down. Chill out. Do less. Devise and record a plan to simplify your life so you'll have the energy you need for change.

Notes

_____

_____

_____

_____

_____

_____

_____

_____

_____

_____

_____

_____

_____

_____

_____

_____

_____

_____

_____

ISOLATION BREEDS ALCOHOL ABUSE

Notes

Physical, psychological and social isolation can cause alcohol abuse. A beer, glass of wine or martini is a party for one. And when you're under the influence, you no longer feel isolated, lonely, bored or unloved.

The party's over. Sitting home alone drinking is not the answer to isolation. Getting out of the house, getting out your feelings and getting out with people you like are.

Look at your life. Are you physically, psychologically or socially isolated? Describe your situation and a plan to break out.

Moderate Drinking Made Easy Workbook

NUMBING NEGATIVE FEELINGS WITH ALCOHOL?

Many people treat stress, anger, depression and anxiety with alcohol. It's true one or two drinks may improve your mood. But getting drunk and medicating yourself with booze on a regular basis doesn't work. You feel even worse when you come down.

It's your responsibility to investigate healthy ways to cope with negative feelings. Start a journal describing your emotions and what issues led to them. Talk to a trusted friend or clergyman about them. Get professional help to sort them out. Acknowledge them and release them, instead of pushing them down until they boil over. Cry, shout, vent, do pushups. Express your feelings in a wholesome, lawful manner, instead of trying to drown them in liquor.

Jot down the emotions or states of mind that trigger your alcohol craving and overdrinking. Then record healthy ways to cope with them and follow through.

Notes

_____

_____

_____

_____

_____

_____

_____

_____

_____

_____

_____

_____

_____

_____

_____

_____

_____

_____

SOOTHE STRESS
AND DRINK LESS

I f you drink when you're stressed, it's time to relax. Practice deep breathing. Exercise. Meditate. Look into self-hypnosis, guided imagery and visualization. Explore progressive muscle relaxation. Listen to music. Practice yoga. Have safe sex. Talk to a professional counselor who specializes in stress reduction.

Write down your stress-reducing plan of action.

DEFEAT DEPRESSION
AND DRINK LESS

I f you drink when you're blue, here are some depression-busting suggestions to clear away the clouds. Exercise. Get more rest. Eat a nutritious, balanced diet - no junk food. Join a support group. Clean house. Stop thinking negative thoughts. Learn to forgive. Seek professional guidance from a person specializing in depression.

What's your plan to chase away the blues? Record it.

Notes

_____

_____

_____

_____

_____

_____

_____

_____

_____

_____

_____

_____

_____

_____

_____

_____

_____

ALLEVIATE ANXIETY AND DRINK LESS

If you drink when you're anxious, here are some tips to calm you down. Exercise. Drink less caffeine. Get more rest. Get a massage. Practice deep breathing and progressive muscle relaxation. Meditate. Look into biofeedback. Talk to a professional specializing in anxiety disorders.

Describe your plan to reduce anxiety in your life.

ALLAY ANGER
AND DRINK LESS

Take a step back when you're heating up. Take a break to cool down. Practice deep breathing. Walk. Vent to a friend. Smile. Seek professional help to deal with your feelings.

Outline your anger management plan.

Notes

_____

_____

_____

_____

_____

_____

_____

_____

_____

_____

_____

_____

_____

_____

_____

_____

_____

PUT THOUGHTS AND WORDS INTO ACTIONS

W e all make grand plans, but often never follow through with them. We think about starting an exercise program, but never get to it. We think about eating more fruits and veggies, then load up on junk food instead. Or we think about finishing that household project, but just never get around to it.

Moderate drinking is no different. How many times have you sworn to yourself, especially when you have a hangover, that you will never lose control and drink too much again? And how many times have you overindulged just days or weeks after you said that to yourself?

It's time to stop thinking about your drinking problem and start doing something about it. No more words, just actions. Take the leap and put your healthy drinking thoughts and words into action. Then, and only then, will you notice a reduction in your alcohol consumption.

What thoughts cross your mind when you're thinking about beating your drinking problem? Record them, then translate them into actions!

Moderate Drinking Made Easy Workbook

LOTS OF LITTLE CHANGES
ADD UP TO BIG ONES

Big changes in your drinking habits are often just an accumulation of lots of little ones. Little changes, like eating while you drink, delaying that first drink of the day by ten minutes or alternating with a non-alcoholic drink, don't seem like a big deal individually. But collectively, they would add up to a huge improvement in your drinking behavior.

Keep making minor adjustments and eventually you'll be thinking and acting like a moderate drinker. It's not rocket science!

List the little changes you plan to make this week. Then keep practicing the ones that work for you.

Notes

_____
_____
_____
_____
_____
_____
_____
_____
_____
_____
_____
_____
_____
_____
_____
_____
_____

THE LESS YOU DRINK, THE LOWER YOUR TOLERANCE

If you're use to drinking a lot of alcohol on a regular basis, you may feel a bit uncomfortable the first few weeks you cut back. That's the bad news. But the good news is you're lowering your tolerance to alcohol and you'll need fewer drinks to feel satisfied. Payoff!

If you consistently reduce your alcohol consumption over several weeks, you'll notice that warm, fuzzy feeling with your very first drink. Your body is adjusting to less liquor and you're becoming more sensitive to it. Not only will you feel the effects of that first glass faster, you'll also notice you don't need as many drinks as you use to have to enjoy yourself. You'll feel satisfied with two - not four - like in the old days. The less you drink, the less alcohol you need. Talk yourself out of another drink with that thought the next time you're facing a challenge.

Are you noticing a difference in your alcohol tolerance after cutting down? Describe it.

WHAT ARE YOUR STATE'S DRUNK DRIVING LAWS AND PENALTIES?

I n California and many other states, you are considered legally drunk at a .08 Blood Alcohol Concentration (BAC) level. In California, most first time DUI offenders are charged with a misdemeanor and may be arrested which can add up to thousands of dollars. Bail is usually set at $500. Car towing and storage could run up to $1,000. Lawyer's fees can cost up to $5,000, but that's not counting the hourly rate they charge if you go to trial. Court fines can run up to $2,500. DUI classes for first-time offenders cost between $500 and $1,000, but repeat offenders pay about $1,600. Your insurance rates will skyrocket for years after an arrest. If you are a repeat offender you may have your license taken away and serve jail time. Not to mention the financial hardship caused by being denied a driver's license for an extended period of time or the public humiliation of being labeled a "drunk driver".

Isn't staying at or under your drink limit worth it? And if you slip and go

Notes

_____

_____

_____

_____

_____

_____

_____

_____

_____

_____

_____

_____

_____

_____

_____

_____

_____

_____

_____

_____

overboard, isn't a twenty dollar, thirty dollar, forty dollar or one hundred dollar cab ride home a bargain, compared to being arrested for drunk driving?

Go to the Department of Motor Vehicles or their website in your state and find out the specific BAC level you're considered to be legally drunk. Then find out the legal penalties for your first DUI or DWI offense, second offense and third offense. Keep in mind, even if your BAC level does not register as being legally drunk, you can still be arrested for being under the influence.

Record your state's drunk driving laws and penalties.

Moderate Drinking Made Easy Workbook

CHANGE IS
99% PERSPIRATION AND
1% INSPIRATION

T homas Alva Edison really said, "Genius is 99% perspiration and 1% inspiration." Substitute change for genius here. You know you're inspired to improve your drinking habits. You're really motivated. That's great. But inspiration is the easy part. The hard part is putting that inspiration to work to make moderate drinking happen.

Edison also said, "I never did anything worth doing by accident, nor did any of my inventions come by accident. They came by hard work." Same goes for moderate drinking. It doesn't come by accident, but only by proactively practicing all of the sensible drinking tips and skills you learn.

Write "Change is challenging, but moderate drinking is worth it" ten times.

Notes

_____

_____

_____

_____

_____

_____

_____

_____

_____

_____

_____

_____

_____

_____

_____

_____

_____

_____

_____

FLEX YOUR
SELF-CONTROL MUSCLES

Self-control, willpower, determination - whatever you want to call it, start cultivating it today. Start with simple exercises, like taking a timeout between drinks or alternating with a mineral water or delaying your happy hour. Succeed at these little changes and you'll grow more confident you can conquer bigger changes down the road.

Jot down your self-control exercises for the coming week.

DON'T YOU JUST LOVE A CHALLENGE?

Over and over, you've demonstrated you've got the right stuff to make your dreams come true. Like putting yourself through college and getting your degree. Or buying your first home on your own. Or surviving a tough childhood to become a successful adult. Cutting down on drinking is a piece of cake, compared to other challenges you've faced and overcome.

Now apply that same "bring it on" attitude that helped you achieve other goals to modifying your drinking habits and attitudes. Bring on that same inner strength, self-control, perseverance and stubbornness to switch to moderate drinking and you'll be drinking like an adult in no time.

What challenges have you overcome in your life? How do they compare to improving your drinking behavior? Write about them.

Notes

_____

_____

_____

_____

_____

_____

_____

_____

_____

_____

_____

_____

_____

_____

_____

_____

_____

_____

_____

_____

GOODBYE PHYSICAL AND PSYCHOLOGICAL HANGOVERS!

When was the last time you had a horrible hangover? The pounding headache, upset stomach, restlessness, irritability. You were probably not only suffering from a physical hangover, but a psychological one as well. Guilt, shame and embarrassment because of your out-of-control drinking. Just think - one whole day of your precious life was lost to an awful hangover.

Or maybe you haven't had a huge hangover lately. But you wake up in the morning feeling tired and slow from too much alcohol. A mild hangover, but a hangover none the less. Another nasty reminder that you didn't manage your drinking.

Next time you're in a partying mood, remember how sick, tired and depressed you made yourself from too much booze. Maybe that thought will deter you from making the same mistake again.

Describe how you felt, physically and psychologically, when you had your last hangover.

Moderate Drinking Made Easy Workbook

HOW DOES LIQUOR FIT INTO
THE BIG PICTURE OF YOUR LIFE?

What's more important to you? A glass of wine or your mate? A martini or your kids? A beer or your job? A gin and tonic or your health? A cosmopolitan or your friends? A scotch and soda or your reputation? A vodka over or your driving record?

Liquor should not be that important in the scheme of your life. And putting it in perspective will discourage heavy, inappropriate drinking and encourage healthy new drinking habits and attitudes. When you put booze in its place, you'll think and act like a moderate drinker naturally.

Jot down all the things in your life that are a lot more important than a cocktail.

Notes

_____

_____

_____

_____

_____

_____

_____

_____

_____

_____

_____

_____

_____

_____

_____

_____

_____

_____

MODERATE DRINKING IS A JOURNEY

Most of us don't change immediately or permanently. We slip back and revisit our old ways several times, we're reminded they weren't so great, then we get back to working on our new improved habits. Eventually, our healthy behaviors win out, become deeply ingrained and we never slip back to our old ways again.

Switching from problem drinking to moderate drinking is a journey and you'll encounter peaks and valleys along the way. You might slip back to your old habits a couple of times, remember why you wanted to change, then get back on track. It's all part of the journey. Remain philosophical, prepare yourself for the long haul and stay true to your moderate drinking commitment - no matter what.

Look into your past. What other changing experiences have you had? Any ups and downs? Describe the process.

Chapter Three:

Moderate Drinking Tips While You Drink

J ohn Locke said, "I have always thought the actions of men are the best interpreters of their thoughts." This is your big opportunity to translate your moderate drinking thoughts into actions.

The only way you'll find out which sensible drinking skills and strategies will work for you is if you try each one at least two times. Keep the ones that work for you - help you to reduce alcohol craving and consumption - and incorporate them into your drinking behavior and lifestyle so you'll never worry about your drinking again.

WHAT IS ONE DRINK?

Notes

_____

_____

_____

_____

_____

_____

_____

_____

_____

_____

_____

_____

_____

_____

_____

_____

_____

_____

I f you're serious about cutting down, you've got to know what "one drink" is and start measuring your drink portions. Five ounces of wine, one and a half ounces of hard liquor and twelve ounces of beer are each considered one drink.

Get your favorite drinking glass. If you drink wine, pour five ounces of water into the glass and mark it. If you drink hard liquor, pour one and a half ounces of water into the glass and mark it. From now on, pour the wine or liquor to that mark to make sure you're only having one drink. If you're a beer drinker you're lucky because most bottles of beer already measure twelve ounces. No cheating!

How much did you consider "one drink" to be in the past? How many drinks were you really having everyday and every week? Jot down the numbers.

Moderate Drinking Made Easy Workbook

KNOW HOW MUCH YOU'LL DRINK BEFORE YOU EVEN START

What's your daily drink limit? Do you have a range? One, two or three? Instead of leaving your drinking to chance and never really knowing how much you'll have when you start drinking, just refer to your daily drink limit or range. Then determine how many cocktails - one, two or three, the max - are right for the event. When you've had your last pre-planned drink, you know you're done for the day. It's that easy.

What's your drink limit or range for a day? What's your drink limit or range for a week? Refresh your memory and write them down.

Notes

_____

_____

_____

_____

_____

_____

_____

_____

_____

_____

_____

_____

_____

_____

_____

_____

_____

_____

_____

IS YOUR DRINKING PLAN IN PLACE?

I t should be if you're drinking right now. You should have decided how many drinks are appropriate for the occasion, how long you'll drink, what skills and strategies you'll use to stay within your drink limit and what you'll say to yourself when it's time to stop drinking.

Put down that drink right now and record your drinking plan before you take another sip.

POLISH YOUR DRINKING ETIQUETTE

What is drinking etiquette? It's polite, moderate drinking. If you're like most drinkers, you probably didn't like the taste of liquor when you first started drinking, so you took small sips. Booze just wasn't that important to you so you drank slowly, nursing that cocktail for a long time. And you never overdid it. You had impeccable drinking manners and you were the perfect moderate drinker.

Over time though, you've gotten sloppy and grown accustom to the taste and effects of alcohol. Now, instead of sipping that first cocktail, you gulp it down. You finish it off in ten or fifteen minutes. And you have another one as fast as you can. Bad habits.

It's time to brush up on your drinking etiquette. To get back to the healthy drinking habits you practiced when you were a novice drinker. First, sip that drink, don't slam it down. Second, put it down between sips. Third, slow down and wait five minutes between sips. Fourth, relax

Notes

_____

_____

_____

_____

_____

_____

_____

_____

_____

_____

_____

_____

_____

_____

_____

_____

_____

_____

_____

_____

_____

and enjoy yourself - there's no need to rush and have another cocktail just because you've finished one.

Write "Sip, don't gulp" ten times. Then do it.

Moderate Drinking Made Easy Workbook

DECISIONS, DECISIONS, DECISIONS

Everyday, all day, each of us has a running conversation in our head - from making the smallest decisions, like what to wear or eat for lunch, to the biggest ones, like where to live or what job to take.

Switching to moderate drinking also involves a series of decisions. To pace yourself or not pace yourself. To eat while you drink or not eat while you drink. To stick to your limit or not stick to your limit. You and the direction of your life depend on the decisions you make. Decide wisely.

Imagine all the decisions you'll make the next time you drink. List them.

Notes

_____

_____

_____

_____

_____

_____

_____

_____

_____

_____

_____

_____

_____

_____

_____

_____

_____

_____

ARE YOU A CONSCIOUS DRINKER?

Conscious drinkers are moderate drinkers who practice polite drinking etiquette and have tons of drinking awareness. Instead of downing one drink after another, they are mindful of each sip and always stay within sensible drinking limits. And they never worry about developing a drinking problem. Payoff!

Are you a conscious drinker? If not, how can you become one? Record your thoughts.

Moderate Drinking Made Easy Workbook

YOU ARE IN CONTROL RIGHT NOW!

Yes, you! It's time for you to feel your power. Your power over liquor that is. When you're drinking and facing your moment of truth - deciding if you should continue or stop drinking - remind yourself alcohol doesn't control you, you control it. You're in charge! You're cleaning up your act and cutting back on booze. And if that other inner voice inside of you pipes up - the one that tells you you're helpless, you have no control and drinking heavily and inappropriately are okay - don't listen to it. It doesn't know what it's talking about.

What does your powerful positive inner voice say when you're tempted to drink recklessly? Describe it.

Notes

_____

_____

_____

_____

_____

_____

_____

_____

_____

_____

_____

_____

_____

_____

_____

_____

_____

_____

WHAT'S YOUR MODERATE DRINKING MANTRA?

What phrase can you silently say to yourself while you're drinking that would help keep you in line? "I never want to worry about my drinking again." "My reputation is more important to me than this martini." "I love healthy living more than liquor." "Booze is just a temporary fix." "My relationship with my family trumps this vodka tonic."

Get busy and dream up a meaningful moderate drinking mantra that would work for you - especially when you've reached your limit and you want another drink.

Record your moderate drinking mantra, then say it to yourself when you're drinking.

TAKE A TIMEOUT FROM EXTERNAL DRINKING CUES

Stop seeing or limit your time with hard drinking buddies. Stop going to or limit your time in clubs or restaurants where you overdrink. Take a break from or cut back on the time you spend at parties, game nights or social occasions that lead to alcohol abuse.

Once you get moderate drinking under your belt, maybe you can increase your exposure to these dangerous cues. But for the time being, taking a timeout from people, places and circumstances that trigger problem drinking is a good idea.

What external drinking cues will you avoid or limit your time around? List them.

Notes

_____

_____

_____

_____

_____

_____

_____

_____

_____

_____

_____

_____

_____

_____

_____

_____

_____

_____

TAKE A TIMEOUT FROM INTERNAL DRINKING CUES TOO . . .

Do emotions, moods or states of mind trip your desire to drink and over-drink? If you get into trouble when you're feeling anxious, angry, frustrated, stressed or depressed, concentrate on relieving those feelings without alcohol.

Start with a regular exercise routine. Clinical research has shown regular exercise alleviates depression, stress and other negative feelings. You might also try relaxation, stress reduction, anger management and hypnosis CDs. And professional counseling is also a possibility. Just a few suggestions to feel better without liquor.

If drinking is your only entertainment when you're bored or lonely, dream up other ways to liven up your life. Join a dating service, volunteer for your favorite charity, take a cooking class or join the Sierra Club. Anything to get you out of the house, socializing and having fun without alcohol.

List the emotions, moods or states of mind that trigger your desire to drink. Then record how you'll handle them without liquor.

Moderate Drinking Made Easy Workbook

LEARN THE ART
OF SAYING NO

Do you know how to say no to a drink? If a friend is always shoving a drink in your hand or the server at your favorite restaurant is always topping off your glass, you'll have to perfect the art of saying no before you can perfect the art of moderate drinking.

Here are a couple of tips to politely refuse another drink. Have a simple excuse up your sleeve. Tell your host you're busy in the morning and want to wake up bright-eyed and bushy-tailed. Or you're trying to lose a few pounds, so you're drinking less. Or you're driving, so you're sticking to a limit. And if you're dining out or at a social event where waiters are keeping your glass filled, just cover it with a napkin - they'll get the message you're fine for the time being.

What reasons can you think up to refuse a drink? List them. Then use them when needed.

Notes

_____

_____

_____

_____

_____

_____

_____

_____

_____

_____

_____

_____

_____

_____

_____

_____

_____

_____

_____

LEARN THE ART OF SAYING YES

Saying yes is almost as important as saying no when practicing the art of moderate drinking. Say yes to a non-alcoholic drink. Say yes to a timeout between drinks. Say yes to your daily drink limit. Say yes to pacing your drink. Say yes to activities that don't involve liquor. Say yes to healthy drinking.

Record all of the sensible drinking strategies and techniques you'll say yes to when you're drinking this week.

CONTROL YOUR
THINKING WHILE DRINKING

Yes, it's possible. When you're drinking and feel tempted to go back to your old ways, catch yourself. Control your thinking and turn negative thoughts into positive ones. Instead of saying to yourself, "I've had a rough day, I don't care about my drink limit and I deserve another drink," turn that counterproductive thought around and say, "I love a challenge, I'm in charge of alcohol and I know I can stay under my limit in spite of a bad day." Replacing negatives with positives will keep you on the straight and narrow. Do it!

What does your negative thinking sound like? What positive thinking do you have in mind to counteract it? Describe them.

ALCOHOL IS NOT YOUR BEST FRIEND!

Notes

_____

_____

_____

_____

_____

_____

_____

_____

_____

_____

_____

_____

_____

_____

_____

_____

_____

_____

_____

How can you convince yourself alcohol is not your best buddy? Perhaps every time you lift a drink to your lips you can say to yourself - out loud or silently - "alcohol is not my best friend." After doing this for a while, you might start believing it!

It's time you made a real best friend. Get out and mingle - take dancing lessons, join a book club, take a cooking class - so you rely less on liquor and more on companionship.

Write "Alcohol is not my best friend" ten times.

Moderate Drinking Made Easy Workbook

VIDEOTAPE YOURSELF DRINKING

Are you ready for your close-up? Next time you're partying, pull out your video recorder and have a friend film you while you're drinking. After every drink, have your pal zoom in and ask you how you're feeling - psychologically and physiologically. Keep the camera rolling - especially if you get higher than you should. Then screen it the next day before you have a drop of alcohol. It might be a sobering experience - especially if you get silly, loud or obnoxious.

Watch your drinking DVD before every high-risk drinking occasion. Could it deter you from going overboard so you stay within your limit and you don't get drunk? It's worth a try.

How do you behave when you stay within your drink limit? How do you behave when you've had one too many? Write about it.

Notes

_____

_____

_____

_____

_____

_____

_____

_____

_____

_____

_____

_____

_____

_____

_____

_____

_____

_____

OBSERVE AND EMULATE
A MODERATE DRINKER

Do you know a person who drinks sensibly all the time, never gets tipsy and never has a problem with alcohol? The perfect moderate drinker? That's the person you want to watch and emulate.

When drinking with them, observe how they sip their glass of wine and pace themselves. Notice how they don't focus on the drink or feel the need to finish it. Count how many drinks they have and pay special attention to when they stop drinking.

From now on, follow their lead and imitate their behavior. Start drinking when they start, sip when they sip and eat if they eat. When they stop drinking, you stop drinking. See what it feels like to be a moderate drinker. You might be clearer on the concept.

Who would you like to emulate? What makes this person a moderate drinker? Describe their drinking style.

SLOW DOWN YOUR DRINKING

Slowing down your drinking is another must if you want to control it. Why? There are lots of reasons, but the most important one is it takes most of us about one hour to metabolize the alcohol in one drink. So if you have more than one drink per hour, you get ahead of yourself, get higher and higher, your judgment becomes impaired and you're incapable of controlling or stopping your drinking.

If you're a fast drinker, start small. Look at your watch and commit to at least twenty minutes for each cocktail. Remember - sip, don't gulp, put the drink down between sips, wait a couple of minutes between sips, distract yourself with pre-planned activities and don't focus on the liquor. If you finish before your twenty minutes are up, don't pour yourself another drink until you've met the time limit. Then and only then, can you have another glass - allowing at least twenty-minutes for that drink as well.

Your ultimate goal should be no more than one drink per hour. If you

Notes

_____

_____

_____

_____

_____

_____

_____

_____

_____

_____

_____

_____

_____

_____

_____

_____

_____

_____

Notes

_____

_____

_____

_____

_____

_____

_____

_____

_____

_____

_____

_____

_____

_____

_____

_____

_____

_____

_____

think that's impossible, gradually work your way up to it. Just add an extra five minutes for each drink each week - the first week you have a twenty minute time limit for each cocktail, the second week you have a twenty-five minute limit and the third week you have a thirty minute limit. Get the idea? If you add an extra five minutes to your drinking time for each drink each week, you'll graduate to sixty minutes per drink within weeks. An effortless way to pace yourself.

Record how long it currently takes you to down each drink - the first, second or third. Then plan and record your future preset drinking times for each week until you reach your "one hour, one drink" goal.

Moderate Drinking Made Easy Workbook

STRETCH YOUR DRINK

T ry this nifty trick when you're drinking. Stretch your mixed drink with more mixer and lots of ice. Start with a bigger glass. Stick to the drink portion for hard liquor - one and a half ounces. Then simply add more ice and mixer to that vodka tonic or scotch and soda. If you're a wine drinker, add a little seltzer water and make a spritzer.

You'll be treating yourself to a bigger drink, it will last longer and you'll be more likely to stay within your time and drink limits. You're fooling yourself into thinking you've got a good-sized drink, but you really don't. The catch is not to add more booze. Whose feeling deprived? Not you!

What drinks can you stretch? List them.

Notes

_____

_____

_____

_____

_____

_____

_____

_____

_____

_____

_____

_____

_____

_____

_____

_____

_____

_____

SWITCH TO
SOMETHING LIGHTER

If you trade in your hard liquor drink, like a martini or manhattan, for beer or wine, you'll be less familiar with the taste and it won't go down as easily as your favorite. You'll slow down, still enjoy yourself and probably drink less. Just one advantage of switching to something lighter.

Another advantage? The alcohol content in beer and wine is not nearly as concentrated as it is in hard liquor. With beer and wine, you get a bigger drink and less effect. Just what you're shooting for.

If you're already a beer or wine drinker, don't bother switching to vodka or scotch or the like. You're already enjoying a lighter alternative.

What's your new, lighter drink of choice? Think about it, jot it down, then stock up.

Moderate Drinking Made Easy Workbook

STRAIGHT LIQUOR IS A NO-NO

Say goodbye to tequila shots, straight scotch, vodka and bourbon. That goes for martinis, long island ice teas and singapore slings too. Drinks that contain pure alcohol, with no mixer, should be off limits from now on.

It's too dangerous to drink straight alcohol on a regular basis. Just a couple of sips and the booze goes to your head, impairs your physiological and psychological reactions and your judgment goes out the window - fast. You're more likely to get drunk, engage in risky behavior and hurt yourself or someone else.

If you still insist on drinking hard liquor, lighten it up with tonic water, club soda, seltzer water, juice or a soft drink. A tamer drink allows you to enjoy yourself, achieve a mild high, but still maintain control.

What drinks will you eliminate and which ones will you lighten up? List them.

Notes

_____

_____

_____

_____

_____

_____

_____

_____

_____

_____

_____

_____

_____

_____

_____

_____

_____

DON'T TOP OFF THAT
DRINK BEFORE IT'S FINISHED

I f you get nervous when your drink is only half full and feel the need to freshen it up before you've finished it, stop. Topping off your drink before it's finished is a bad idea and the sign of a problem drinker.

A moderate drinker, who doesn't have a problem with alcohol, wouldn't dream of refilling their cocktail until it's gone. They don't obsess about having a full glass and only consider having another drink when they're done.

Next time you're looking at a disappearing drink, feel a little panicky and want to replenish it, remind yourself of how silly you're being. Describe your feelings. Then get over it.

START HAPPY HOUR
WITH A SOFT DRINK

Get your cocktail hour off to a roaring non-alcoholic start with your favorite mineral water, soda or juice. Make sure you're well-stocked, so you have no excuses for drinking "soft," instead of "hard" - at least at the beginning of your happy hour.

You'll be changing your old drinking pattern, delaying your drinking and spending less time on liquor. Such a simple alteration to control your drinking and build your self-control!

List the non-alcoholic beverages you'll keep on hand. Then put them to good use.

Notes

_____

_____

_____

_____

_____

_____

_____

_____

_____

_____

_____

_____

_____

_____

_____

_____

_____

_____

TIE A STRING
AROUND YOUR FINGER

Sometimes, when you're drinking, especially when you're partying with friends, it's so easy to get caught up in the moment and forget all about your commitment to moderate drinking. You're having a great time and controlling your drinking is the last thing on your mind.

Perhaps a little reminder - like tying a string on your finger - will help. Every time you see or feel that string, you'll remember your commitment, your drink limit and your payoffs. Do it!

If a string wouldn't work for you, what would? Think about it, write it down and do it every time you drink.

THAT EXTRA DRINK
GOES IN THE SINK

Okay, you blew it. You just poured yourself another drink that will put you over your limit. And now you regret it.

Here's the solution. When you pour one too many and have a change of heart, dump that extra drink in the sink. You can rectify your mistake in a split second. Quick, painless and no second thoughts.

When was the last time you could have employed this simple technique to stay within your drink limit? Write about it.

Notes

_____

_____

_____

_____

_____

_____

_____

_____

_____

_____

_____

_____

_____

_____

_____

_____

_____

_____

DELAY THAT DRINK

Notes

Delaying your first drink and successive drinks is an easy self-control baby step that will reduce your drinking time. Say it's a little after five and that happy hour mentality has kicked in. Instead of inhaling that first cocktail immediately, look at your watch, wait ten minutes and cool off. Get lost in a distracting activity - have a soft drink, call a friend, walk the dog, fix dinner, water the plants, visualize. Time will fly and before you know it, you may have delayed even longer than ten minutes. Then and only then, allow yourself that first cocktail. Plan on putting off second or third drinks by ten minutes as well.

It feels so good to be in control! When you get good at ten minute timeouts, stretch it to fifteen, then twenty minutes.

Write "I'll take a ten minute time-out before every drink" ten times. Then do it.

DON'T TANK UP
BEFORE YOU GO OUT

Downing drinks at home to save money on the liquor bill when you go out is the result of dangerous drinking thinking - illogical thinking that encourages you to drink too much, too fast and inappropriately. Even though it seems logical to try and save a buck on booze at a restaurant or club, having two, three or four cocktails at home first, then having more when you're out spells DRUNK.

A responsible drinker would never dream of doing this. If they had any alcohol before a night on the town, they'd only have one or two.

When was the last time you tanked up before going out? Record how much you drank that night - if you can remember. Then write about how you'll handle yourself in the future when you're faced with the same situation.

Notes

_____

_____

_____

_____

_____

_____

_____

_____

_____

_____

_____

_____

_____

_____

_____

_____

_____

FOOD AND LIQUOR MIX

Notes

Eating before and during drinking can't be over-emphasized if you want to improve your drinking habits. Food raises and stabilizes your blood sugar levels - enhancing your mood and decreasing your desire to drink. It also protects your stomach lining from the harmful effects of alcohol and slows the absorption of it into your system so it doesn't go to your head - making it easier for you to pace your drinking and stick to your limit. Delicious reasons to eat before and during drinking!

Make a shopping list of your favorite snacks. Include nutritional nibbles, like low-fat cheese, whole grain crackers, fruits, veggies and nuts. Stock up on these goodies so you'll have no excuse to not eat while you drink.

Moderate Drinking Made Easy Workbook

FOCUS ON PEOPLE, CONVERSATION AND ACTIVITY - NOT ALCOHOL

Have you ever blown a social drinking party? Where you drank too much and lost it - embarrassing yourself, alienating your friends and ruining your reputation.

Never blow a social drinking party again. Stop focusing on that precious drink and start focusing on the people, conversation and activities at the event. Catch up on what others are doing, eat, network, dance, tell jokes, play the piano, sing, do magic tricks. You'll not only drink less, you'll be the life of the party!

What social drinking occasions are coming up for you in the next week, the next month? How will you handle them? Record your plans.

Notes

_____

_____

_____

_____

_____

_____

_____

_____

_____

_____

_____

_____

_____

_____

_____

_____

_____

_____

WHAT SHOULD YOU ASK YOURSELF WHEN FACING YOUR MOMENT OF TRUTH?

Remember? Your moment of truth is when you're deciding if you should start or stop drinking. If you have a hard time deciding when to stop drinking, here's a simple, objective method to take the guesswork out of your decision. Ask yourself these three questions:

Have I reached my limit?
Am I high enough?
Do I really want another drink?

If you answer yes to one of the first two questions, you're done. If you answer no to the first two questions, but yes to the third, you can have another drink. Wasn't that easy?

Write down each question five times and ask them before every drink from now on.

Moderate Drinking Made Easy Workbook

HALT!

D o you drink when you're hungry, angry, lonely or tired? HALT! Stop and think about this clever acronym coined by Alcoholics Anonymous and you might reconsider that cocktail.

HALT - whenever you're experiencing any one of the above physiological or psychological states and you want a drink. Take a step back, rethink the reasons behind your need to drink and remedy the situation without liquor. Eat, chill out, socialize or go to bed, instead of having a martini.

Make HALT signs and post them on your nightstand, fridge, in your car or on your liquor cabinet. Just little reminders to raise your drinking awareness and eliminate inappropriate drinking.

Look at your drinking diary entries for the last two weeks and record how many times you started or continued to drink because you were hungry, angry, lonely or tired.

Notes

_____

_____

_____

_____

_____

_____

_____

_____

_____

_____

_____

_____

_____

_____

_____

_____

_____

COMPROMISE WITH YOURSELF

So many drinkers give up on controlled drinking the second they're tempted to go over their drink limit. They think just having the desire to continue drinking makes them a failure. They give up, get drunk and all is lost.

Compromising with yourself could help. When you want to continue drinking, but you know you shouldn't, allow yourself a half of a drink. A half drink will satisfy the need, but only put you a little over your limit. So instead of ditching moderate drinking altogether and getting smashed, you're still exercising a little self-control and managing alcohol with a modest compromise.

Think about times when you've had an intense desire to continue drinking, but you've reached your limit. Do you think compromising would have helped? Record your thoughts. Then try it the next time you're feeling challenged.

PASSING UP THAT DRINK IS NOT BRAIN SURGERY!

Think of all the tough challenges you've overcome in your life. Stopping smoking? Getting yourself out of debt? Healing from a devastating loss or serious illness? Passing up that third or fourth drink is child's play, compared to the huge obstacles you've conquered in the past!

List the greatest accomplishments of your life. Then imagine how easy it will be to drink less.

Notes

_____

_____

_____

_____

_____

_____

_____

_____

_____

_____

_____

_____

_____

_____

_____

_____

_____

LEAVE A LITTLE
AND FEEL GREAT

When you drink, do you think you must finish every last drop of that cocktail no matter what? To get a little higher, not to waste liquor or just out of habit? Yes - we've all been taught "waste not, want not". But this saying doesn't apply to alcohol.

From now on, try something different. Don't finish your drink a couple of times a week. Just put it down and walk away or pour it down the drain. When you do, you'll be making an empowering statement to yourself and alcohol: you can take it or leave it. You'll be putting liquor in its place, minimizing its importance in your life and taking back the power it has taken away from you.

How do you feel when you leave a little? Write about your feelings.

THINK SHORT-TERM

L ike right now - while you're drinking. Don't lose yourself in the euphoria of the alcohol, forget about your commitment and drinking plan, give up control and let the booze take over. For the time being, you've got to stay on your toes and pay close attention to everything you think and do around liquor.

It won't always be like this. Eventually, you'll get better and better at managing your drinking and sticking to your limit. And it will feel natural. It'll just take some time and practice.

When was the last time you got caught up in the moment with that cocktail and overdrank? Describe it. And don't let it happen again.

Notes

A LITTLE CONTROL IS
IS BETTER THAN NONE

Uh, oh. You're drinking, you're high and you're tempted to let loose. Drinking as much and as fast as you can, like in days past.

Bad idea. You'll pay for that decision in more ways than one. In the morning you'll have a hangover, regret what you said and did, feel bad about yourself and try to repair the damage.

The next time you want to throw caution to the wind and exceed your limit, exercise just a little self-control and avoid this ugly morning-after scenario. The lesson here is you don't have to get drunk if you go over your limit!

Write "A little control is better than none" ten times. Then act on it when the time comes!

Moderate Drinking Made Easy Workbook

THINK OF YOUR REPUTATION . . .

Your good name. One of your most precious possessions. How often have you tarnished it by drinking too much and behaving like an idiot?

When you reach for a drink, remind yourself a lot is at stake. Not just health, relationship, money and legal problems. As if that wasn't enough. Your precious reputation - what people think of you - is also at risk. And once you lose your reputation to alcohol, it could take years to recover it.

Has booze soiled your reputation? Write about it.

Notes

_____

_____

_____

_____

_____

_____

_____

_____

_____

_____

_____

_____

_____

_____

_____

_____

_____

DRINK LIKE AN ADULT!

Stuck in the old adolescent bingeing phase? The one you learned in high school or college? Where you and your pals got together and drank as much and as fast as you could until you were drunk? It's time to grow up and start drinking like an adult.

We're all saddled with drinking habits and attitudes we learned from family and friends. We didn't know any better. Now you know better. You're all grown up, you're an adult, so start acting like one around liquor.

Are you still drinking like a kid? If so, record the last time you binged. Then describe how you felt and how you felt about yourself the next day.

Moderate Drinking Made Easy Workbook

HOW MUCH TIME DO YOU SPEND DRINKING?

Y ou are a dynamic, multi-faceted individual with lots of living to do. Drinking more than an hour or two a day is a waste of your precious time. If you're risking your family, friends, job, financial security and freedom, because of all the time you obsess about alcohol, drink it and recover from it, you need to put booze back in its place - just a small complement to your big life.

How many hours a day do you drink? How can you cut down on your drinking time? Record your plan.

Notes

_____

_____

_____

_____

_____

_____

_____

_____

_____

_____

_____

_____

_____

_____

_____

_____

_____

_____

_____

DON'T DRINK, MEDITATE

Your spiritual self is a place where perfect peace and joy reside - untouched by external events or internal emotions. Here's a simple meditation to help you tap into your spiritual side so you rely on alcohol less and less . . .

Get comfortable - lie down or sit quietly and close your eyes. Take a deep breath, hold it for five seconds, then slowly exhale. While you exhale, concentrate on releasing stress, negative feelings and physical tension. Relax with this deep breathing exercise for five minutes. Inevitably, your mind will wander. Don't fight it. However, when you do find yourself wandering, refocus on slow, deep breathing and letting go of negative thoughts.

After five minutes, hopefully you'll reach a quieter place inside - your spiritual self - where you feel calm and free from the physical world. When you achieve this totally relaxed and peaceful state, enjoy! Take another five or ten minutes to think about absolutely nothing. When you're ready to come back to the real world, reflect on how light, bright and energized you feel as you continue your day.

This meditation could be just the beginning of a spiritual journey for you. One which replaces your need for alcohol with a feeling of serenity. The next time that cocktail is calling, try quiet meditation instead.

Reflect on how tapping into your calm, spiritual side might affect your alcohol craving and consumption.

Notes

_____

_____

_____

_____

_____

_____

_____

_____

_____

_____

_____

_____

_____

_____

_____

_____

_____

IS THAT EXTRA DRINK
REALLY WORTH IT?

L ook at the big picture of your life. Your family and friends. Your good health. Your reputation. Feeling good about yourself and the direction of your life. The list is endless. Then think about losing it all if you continue to drink too much.

Is that extra drink really worth it? Worth risking your health, relationships, reputation and self-esteem? If you say yes, you're hopeless and need to stop drinking. If you say no, act on your internal dialogue and have a soft drink instead of a beer.

Write "An extra drink is not worth it" ten times. Then say it to yourself whenever you want an extra drink.

ROLL WITH THE PUNCHES

So you're getting good at pre-planning your drinking behavior and you're actually following through with fantastic results. You're drinking less!

Most of the time, sticking to your drinking plan is easy. But then, the unexpected happens. The drinking party doesn't go as you anticipated and your plan doesn't work. Don't stress. Just expect the unexpected. Roll with the punches and alter your drinking plan so you can stay within your drink limit.

If friends have you over for a drink or two and it turns into dinner, it's your responsibility to spontaneously devise a three or four hour drinking plan to replace the one or two hour plan you started with. Give yourself a stirring payoff pep talk, drink slower, alternate with non-alcoholic beverages and have coffee and dessert instead of another drink. You should have dozens of behavior management skills up your sleeve to use at a moments notice.

When was the last time your drinking plan didn't work out

Notes

_____

_____

_____

_____

_____

_____

_____

_____

_____

_____

_____

_____

_____

_____

_____

_____

_____

_____

because of unforeseen events? Describe the party and how you could have revised your plan to stay within your drink limit.

WHO'S THE BOSS?

You or alcohol? You are and don't forget it! It's especially important for you to remember you're the boss while you're drinking. You control alcohol, not the other way around. Anytime you're under the influence, keep this empowering thought in mind.

Write "I'm the boss, not alcohol" ten times. Then start to believe it.

Notes

_____

_____

_____

_____

_____

_____

_____

_____

_____

_____

_____

_____

_____

_____

_____

_____

_____

_____

_____

BYE BYE
ALCOHOL CRAVING

When you're drinking and you want to continue to drink, isn't it comforting to know your desire to keep on drinking will fade with just the passage of time? Wait it out and focus on something else - a snack, socializing, reading the paper, preparing for that afternoon meeting - and you'll forget all about it in five or ten minutes. Be patient and you'll feel better in no time. So long, alcohol craving.

Reflect on and write about waiting out your cravings while you're drinking.

Moderate Drinking Made Easy Workbook

HAVE THE LAST LAUGH
ON ALCOHOL CRAVING

Imagine you're having a red-hot craving and you just can't shake it. Nothing is working, not even waiting it out. How about a little humor to cool you off? Have a good laugh at yourself and how worked up you're getting over a silly little cocktail. You'll defuse that powerful urge in no time and minimize the importance of liquor in your life.

Have a giggle every time you face an intense craving and record your thoughts - about craving and laughing.

Notes

_____

_____

_____

_____

_____

_____

_____

_____

_____

_____

_____

_____

_____

_____

_____

_____

_____

THE MORE YOU STICK TO YOUR LIMIT, THE LESS ALCOHOL YOU NEED TO GET HIGH

I t's true! If you stick to your drink limit, the less tolerant you'll be to alcohol, the less alcohol you'll need to get high and the less you'll drink.

If you've been drinking too much on a regular basis, you've built up a tolerance to booze. But if you reduce your alcohol consumption for just a couple of weeks, two things will happen. First, you'll lower your tolerance to liquor. And second, you won't need as much alcohol to get that warm, fuzzy feeling so it will be easier for you to stick to your drink limit. Hang in there.

What physiological and psychological changes have you noticed the first two weeks of cutting down? Describe them.

Moderate Drinking Made Easy Workbook

MOCKTAILS MIGHT BE JUST AS MUCH FUN

Feeling deprived because you're sticking to your drink limit? Treat yourself to a mocktail, instead of a real cocktail, and keep the party going. Here are recipes for four pretenders, thanks to Kathy Hamlin, a professional bartender. They taste so good you'll forget they don't have any booze in them!

I'll Fake Manhattan
- 1 ½ ounces each of cranberry and orange juice
- Two dashes of orange bitters
- A dash of grenadine and lemon juice

Stir over ice.
Serve in a chilled cocktail glass.

Margarita
- 2 ounces sweet and sour mix
- Splash each of lime and orange juice

Blend with ice until smooth.
Serve in a salt-rimmed glass.
Garnish with a lime wedge.

Notes

_____
_____
_____
_____
_____
_____
_____
_____
_____
_____
_____
_____
_____
_____
_____
_____
_____
_____
_____
_____

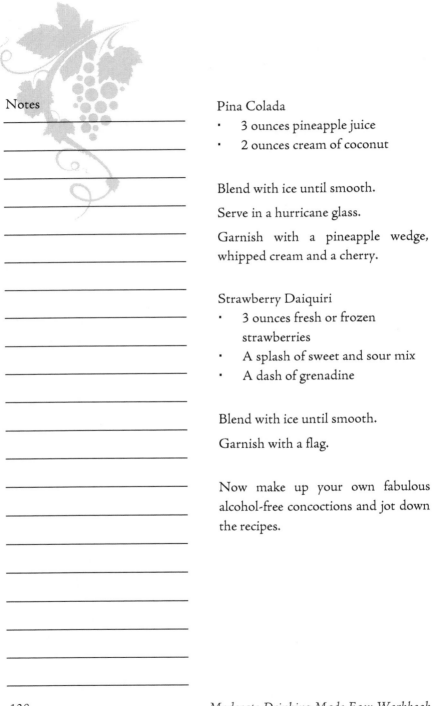

Notes

Pina Colada
- 3 ounces pineapple juice
- 2 ounces cream of coconut

Blend with ice until smooth.

Serve in a hurricane glass.

Garnish with a pineapple wedge, whipped cream and a cherry.

Strawberry Daiquiri
- 3 ounces fresh or frozen strawberries
- A splash of sweet and sour mix
- A dash of grenadine

Blend with ice until smooth.

Garnish with a flag.

Now make up your own fabulous alcohol-free concoctions and jot down the recipes.

Moderate Drinking Made Easy Workbook

LITTLE HELPERS MIGHT KEEP YOU ON TRACK

How about getting a breathalyzer or alcohol testing kit to keep you on track? They measure how high you are - your Blood Alcohol Concentration (BAC) level - so you can decide if you should slow down or stop drinking or if it's safe to get behind the wheel.

Testing yourself can also be a learning experience. When you measure your BAC level after one, two or three drinks, take note of the physiological and psychological changes you're experiencing. Just beginning to feel relaxed, physically and mentally, at .02 BAC? Is stress and body tension melting away? Feeling friendlier and more talkative at .04 BAC? A bit impaired, physically and mentally, at .06 BAC?

Sensitizing yourself to body and brain changes when you're high will increase your drinking awareness and, with time, you'll be able to identify certain feelings associated with specific BAC levels so you'll automatically know when to stop

Notes

_____

_____

_____

_____

_____

_____

_____

_____

_____

_____

_____

_____

_____

_____

_____

_____

_____

_____

_____

drinking. Then, and only then, are you allowed to stop counting drinks!

List the physiological and psychological changes you experience at different BAC levels every time you drink in the next two weeks.

_____

_____

_____

_____

_____

_____

_____

_____

_____

_____

_____

_____

_____

_____

_____

_____

_____

_____

_____

WHAT VOID DOES
ALCOHOL FILL IN YOUR LIFE?

Why do so many people get into trouble with alcohol? Because they look to liquor to fill a void in their life. Maybe it's loneliness, maybe boredom, maybe it's because they don't feel good about themselves or others. Whatever the reason, being under the influence closes the gap.

Now, while you're drinking, before every drink say to yourself, "alcohol is not love" or "alcohol is not a therapist" or "alcohol is not an ego builder" - whatever applies to you. Then remind yourself that booze is just a quick fix. It's not meant to fill social or psychological voids in your life.

What void does alcohol fill in your life? What will you say to yourself every time you think about lifting a glass to your lips? Write it down.

Notes

_____

_____

_____

_____

_____

_____

_____

_____

_____

_____

_____

_____

_____

_____

_____

_____

_____

_____

HAVE YOU CALCULATED YOUR BAC LEVELS?

_____
_____
_____
_____
_____
_____
_____
_____
_____
_____
_____
_____
_____
_____
_____
_____
_____
_____
_____
_____
_____
_____

Did you get a DUI, DWI or Blood Alcohol Concentration (BAC) level chart to see how many drinks it takes to get you mildly high, tipsy or drunk over a one, two or three hour period? If you haven't, stop drinking right now and look into it. This information should be available at your state's Department of Motor Vehicles or on their website. It can also be accessed at http://www.dmv.ca.gov/pubs/hdbk/pgs72duichart.htm, the California Department of Motor Vehicles website.

Record the drink numbers. Crucial information - especially if you insist on drinking and driving.

ARE YOU A GOOD ROLE MODEL AROUND LIQUOR?

Teaching your kids how to drink conservatively and appropriately is more valuable than the family jewels. You're the first person in your child's life to show them how to behave around alcohol - they're always observing how much and how often you drink - and like it or not, they're bound to emulate your drinking style.

When they see you drinking in moderation and treating liquor as a complement to a healthy lifestyle, you'll be giving them one of the greatest gifts of all: a lifetime free from alcohol abuse. But if you're a slave to an alcohol habit, drink too much and too often, you're setting them up for a drinking problem.

Next time you pour a tall one, are your kids watching? Think about how your drinking affects your children and their future. By the way, don't bother trying to sneak it, they'll pick right up on that.

What drinking habits are you passing on to your kids? Write about them.

Notes

_____

_____

_____

_____

_____

_____

_____

_____

_____

_____

_____

_____

_____

_____

_____

_____

_____

_____

DRINKING 101

You're the student, teacher and principal all rolled into one for Drinking 101 - an exercise meant to hone your moderate drinking skills and mindset.

Do your homework (devise your drinking plan) before class (your drinking event). How many drinks will you have? How long will you drink? Will you pace yourself and watch the clock? Eat while you drink? Focus on your payoffs? Remind yourself how great you'll feel in the morning if you behave?

Your final? A drinking occasion, alone or with friends, where you put your healthy drinking skills and strategies to the test - proving you can drink sensibly.

When's your next class? Jot down your homework.

RESPECT THE POWER OF BOOZE

A beer or glass of wine. A shot of tequila or scotch. A pina colada. It all sounds so innocent. But it's not. Two or three of these innocent little drinks and your self-control evaporates, your judgment becomes impaired, you are incapable of making rational decisions, your commitment to moderate drinking goes out the window and you become a danger to yourself and others.

You need to recognize and respect the power of alcohol and the huge influence it can have on you. The more you respect it, the less you'll abuse it.

Reflect on the power of alcohol and record your thoughts.

Notes

_____

_____

_____

_____

_____

_____

_____

_____

_____

_____

_____

_____

_____

_____

_____

_____

_____

ALCOHOL, I CAN TAKE YOU OR LEAVE YOU

From here on out, before every cocktail, before every sip, look at that drink and say, "alcohol, I can take you or leave you". Say it out loud or silently to yourself. It might just penetrate your subconscious and lead you to the conscious thought that booze really isn't that important to you and you really can take it or leave it. What have you got to lose? A drinking problem! Even if you don't believe it at first, you might over time.

Write "alcohol, I can take you or leave you" ten times. Then start to believe it!

REMEMBER THE MODERATE DRINKING FORMULA?

If you're not following through with your safe drinking plan when you're drinking, you're either too high, you don't have a strong enough commitment to moderate drinking or you're not motivated enough to put your healthy drinking skills into action. Commitment, motivation and sensible drinking actions equal moderate drinking - the moderate drinking formula.

Are you following through with your safe drinking plan while you're drinking? If not, why not? Record your thoughts.

Notes

_____

_____

_____

_____

_____

_____

_____

_____

_____

_____

_____

_____

_____

_____

_____

_____

_____

_____

_____

REMEMBER? APPROPRIATE DRINKING IS THE ANSWER

Notes
_____
_____
_____
_____
_____
_____
_____
_____
_____
_____
_____
_____
_____
_____
_____
_____
_____
_____
_____
_____

Have you been drinking appropriately? Appropriate drinking is drinking that's suited to the occasion. It usually involves food, friends and good times and you never drink too much or too fast. Inappropriate drinking, on the other hand, is drinking that is not suited to the occasion. It's drinking too much, too fast and for no good reason.

Every time you lift that glass to your lips you should be asking yourself, "Is this appropriate drinking?". Make it a part of your drinking routine. It might keep you in line.

What drinking events are coming up in the next week? Are they appropriate drinking occasions? Why? Why not? Describe them.

ARE YOU LISTENING TO YOUR PAYOFF PEP TALK?

Have you recorded your payoff pep talk? If not, get busy and do it right now. Then put it to good use. Pop it in your CD or cassette player and listen to it everyday - whether you're drinking or not. Listen to it before and while you're drinking too. And play it at night when you're drifting off to sleep. It will keep you focused and on track.

Refresh your memory and write down your reasons for sticking to sensible drinking.

Notes

_____

_____

_____

_____

_____

_____

_____

_____

_____

_____

_____

_____

_____

_____

_____

_____

REMEMBER YOUR END OF THE DRINKING DAY RITUAL?

Are you following through with your "end of the drinking day" ritual? You know, the pre-planned snack or activity that signals to you you've reached your drink limit and you're done drinking for the day? Here's a friendly reminder to follow through with it, otherwise it's just a useless concept.

What's your "end of the drinking day" pleasure? Jot it down.

THE SMALLEST ACTION
IS BETTER THAN
THE BIGGEST INTENTION

The smallest positive change you make is better than the biggest intention you never follow through with. In fact, all of your grand plans to drink less are worthless if you don't act on them. Start practicing what you preach. You'll have moderate drinking to show for it!

What positive changes will you incorporate into your drinking routine in the next week? List them.

Notes

_____

_____

_____

_____

_____

_____

_____

_____

_____

_____

_____

_____

_____

_____

_____

_____

_____

_____

STOP AND SMELL THE ROSES

Research shows your sense of smell is associated with your mood and certain odors can elicit feelings of well-being. It follows that if you smell a scent you love, the better you'll feel and the less you'll want alcohol. An excellent excuse to treat yourself to a dozen roses.

Experiment with different fragrances. We're not just talking about refined colognes or perfumes, but natural oil essences from plants like peppermint, lavender, vanilla and sage. When craving strikes, place a drop or two of your favorite scent above your upper lip and get a good whiff.

Try out different fragrances at the herb store and perfume counter. What scents affect your mood? Which ones are uplifting? Which ones decrease your desire to drink? List the ones that work for you.

LOOK FORWARD
AND REMAIN POSITIVE

When you're drinking, stay upbeat and look to the future. Don't dwell on mistakes you made in the past. That's counterproductive. With a positive attitude you're more likely to stay in control and within your limit.

Write "My goal is a life free from alcohol abuse" ten times.

Notes

_____

_____

_____

_____

_____

_____

_____

_____

_____

_____

_____

_____

_____

_____

_____

_____

_____

_____

SO LONG, WORRIES

Not having a hangover in the morning. Not having to apologize for the things you said or did. Not ruining your reputation. Not being concerned about alcohol-related health problems. Not being fired or arrested. You'll eliminate a lot of worries if you eliminate problem drinking.

Now, while you're drinking, record the problems you won't worry about if you drink moderately.

Chapter Four:

Moderate Drinking Tips After You Drink

B en Franklin said, "Energy and persistence conquer all things." Now dig in, regroup and rethink your attitudes and actions around alcohol with moderate drinking tips after you drink. The more you know, the more your energy and persistence will pay off!

REWARD YOURSELF FOR A JOB WELL DONE!

Acknowledging and rewarding yourself for staying within your drink limits is essential to make a permanent improvement in your drinking habits. It's called positive reinforcement! It reinforces the moderate drinking skills and attitudes you're learning and builds your self-control and self-confidence.

Rewarding yourself for a drinking job well done could be a psychological pat on the back - a passionate, positive self-talk, like telling yourself how wonderful you are for passing up that extra drink. Or it could be a tangible one, like a chocolate truffle, a new outfit or a trip to Hawaii. However you decide to treat yourself, follow through and savor your successes.

List five rewards you have in mind when you stick to your daily and weekly drink limits.

Moderate Drinking Made Easy Workbook

WHAT'S STANDING BETWEEN YOU AND MODERATE DRINKING?

Your lack of commitment? Your lack of motivation? Your inability to follow through with healthy drinking skills and strategies? Whatever the problem is, isolate it and fix it.

Describe what's keeping you from meeting your sensible drinking goal and how you'll deal with it so it no longer stands in your way.

Notes

_____

_____

_____

_____

_____

_____

_____

_____

_____

_____

_____

_____

_____

_____

_____

_____

_____

_____

_____

GETTING UP AGAIN IS PART OF THE MODERATE DRINKING JOURNEY

Becoming a moderate drinker doesn't happen overnight. There will be ups and downs. And it's how you handle those ups and downs that will determine your success at sensible drinking.

When you slip and drink too much, don't beat yourself up and give up. Get back in the game immediately. If you don't, you've lost and liquor has won. You win when you're not defeated by a slip or two, you reaffirm your commitment to moderate drinking and you get right back on track.

How do you feel when you go over your drink limit? Record your thoughts. Then write down what you'll say to yourself to get back in the game.

FOLLOW THE MODERATE DRINKING FORMAT EVERY WEEK

At the beginning of every week, it's time to take stock, see where you've been and see where you're headed. That means looking over your drinking diary for the past week and analyzing your successes and challenges. And looking at the coming week, predicting when and where you'll drink and pre-planning your drinking behavior for those occasions. Analyzing past drinking events and pre-planning for future ones is the moderate drinking format you'll follow every week from now on.

Successes are when you stay within your daily drink limit and do not exceed a .06 Blood Alcohol Concentration (BAC) level. Challenges are when you exceed your limit and go over a .06 BAC level.

When reviewing the past week, first give yourself a pat on the back for your successes - reinforcing what you did right. Then ask yourself what skills and strategies helped you to stick to your limit. Pre-planning, watching the clock, eating, alternating? Take note of what worked for you, so you can include these skills in future drinking plans.

Notes

_____

_____

_____

_____

_____

_____

_____

_____

_____

_____

_____

_____

_____

_____

_____

_____

_____

_____

_____

_____

_____

Notes
_____

_____

_____

_____

_____

_____

_____

_____

_____

_____

_____

_____

_____

_____

_____

_____

_____

_____

Next, look at the most challenging drinking times over the last week. The ones where you drank too much. What factors led you to overdrink? Pinpoint them, then brainstorm ways you could handle differently so they won't happen again. Hopefully, the next time you'll stick to your limit.

Then, look at the week ahead. What days do you think drinking might come up? At home, dinner out, a social occasion? Again, make specific plans for each event. Being armed with a drinking plan of action works!

Review your drinking diary for the past week and record your successes and challenges and what led to them. Then record drinking events you anticipate in the coming week and your plans to manage them.

Moderate Drinking Made Easy Workbook

WHERE WILL YOU BE
TEN YEARS FROM NOW?

Alive? Alone? Divorced? Un-employed? Broke? Home-less? No driver's license? Estranged from your kids, family and friends? Suffering from alcohol-related health problems? Have an arrest record for drunk driving, public drunkenness or domestic violence? Attending AA meetings to get clean and sober? So many unpleasant alternatives await you if you don't do something about your drinking right now.

Where will you be ten years from now if you continue down your problem drinking path? List the problems you could face if you don't get a grip on your drinking.

Notes

_____

_____

_____

_____

_____

_____

_____

_____

_____

_____

_____

_____

_____

_____

_____

_____

_____

_____

_____

DOES YOUR EXCUSE TO DRINK STILL EXIST?

You may have started drinking heavily for one reason and continued to drink heavily even after that problem was resolved. Think about it. When did you develop a drinking problem? What issues, emotions or stressors led you to overdrinking in the first place? Have they been resolved, but you're still drinking like there's no tomorrow?

If the reasons that drove you to drink in the first place have been settled, but you're still drinking like they haven't been, wise up. You no longer have an excuse to keep abusing alcohol! It's time to own up, stop this old drinking pattern and put it behind you, along with the problems that started it.

Record the issues that once drove you to drink but no longer exist.

STOP THINKING ABOUT CHANGE AND DO IT!

Any change in drinking behavior happens in two stages: first, the thinking stage and then, the doing stage. In the thinking stage, you imagine how great your life will be without so much alcohol and you plan the changes you'll make. In the doing stage, all of the thinking and planning you've done to clean up your drinking act are translated into actions.

At some point, you have to stop "thinking" about change and "do" change. That's how change happens. And that's when you'll see a real reduction in your alcohol consumption. Keep that in mind the next time you're facing your moment of truth - when you're deciding if you should start or stop drinking.

Describe your thinking and doing stages in your quest to drink less.

Notes

_____

_____

_____

_____

_____

_____

_____

_____

_____

_____

_____

_____

_____

_____

_____

_____

_____

RELAX, THE FIRST COUPLE
OF WEEKS ARE THE HARDEST

I f you can successfully cut down on your drinking for a couple of weeks, you've proven you can do it. Drink less! And you can do it the rest of your life if you really want to.

Take comfort in knowing the worst is probably over. Yes, there will still be times when you want to drink over your limit. You're not out of the woods yet. But you've proven you can control your drinking. And you can put the doubts and fears you had about it to rest.

Write about how you felt - good and bad - during the first two weeks of cutting down.

Moderate Drinking Made Easy Workbook

THE LESS YOU DRINK, THE LESS IMPORTANT ALCOHOL WILL BECOME

Maybe not at first. Maybe you'll focus on alcohol even more if you feel deprived. Seems like the more you want to manage or cut back on something, like food, alcohol or tobacco, the more you want it. It's just human nature.

But once you experience the joys of moderate drinking and appreciate how good you look and feel, the less you'll care about booze. It will no longer be the focus of your life and chances are you won't revert back to your old problem drinking ways.

Describe the importance or unimportance of alcohol in your life - before you cut down and after you cut down.

Notes

_____

_____

_____

_____

_____

_____

_____

_____

_____

_____

_____

_____

_____

_____

_____

_____

_____

_____

WHAT'S YOUR PSYCHOLOGICAL TOLERANCE TO ALCOHOL?

W e've talked about physical tolerance to alcohol. Needing more and more alcohol to get high. Now let's talk about psychological tolerance to alcohol - deeply ingrained bad habits around liquor that are hard to break.

You'll be happy to know the more you practice your brand new moderate drinking skills and strategies, the more successful you'll be at lowering your psychological tolerance. Keep working on your healthy drinking habits and your need to engage in your old destructive drinking pattern will decrease, your sensible new drinking behavior will take hold and your psychological tolerance will diminish.

On a scale from one to ten, how strong is your psychological tolerance to alcohol - with one being the weakest and ten being the strongest? Record it.

STOP HIDING BEHIND BOOZE

No more hiding bottles. No more hiding from behind bottles. No more suppressing your feelings with alcohol. No more drinking your life away.

Allowing yourself and others to know who you really are and what you really think and feel will eliminate your need for booze. Are you up to the task?

What are you hiding from with liquor? Describe it.

Notes

_____

_____

_____

_____

_____

_____

_____

_____

_____

_____

_____

_____

_____

_____

_____

_____

_____

_____

THINK COMMITMENT
WHEN CHALLENGED

Feeling pulled back to your old ways at times? Start anew and recommit yourself. Remain positive, revive your motivation and work even harder to stay within your daily and weekly drink limits with safe drinking skills and strategies.

Refresh your memory and write about your strong commitment to moderate drinking.

WHAT DOES ALCOHOL HELP YOU COPE WITH?

A lousy relationship? Financial problems? A job you hate? If you drink to cope, it's time to face the issues bothering you, instead of trying to drink them away.

Liquor is not a permanent solution to dealing with difficult people or situations. You have to either give up on them, manage them better or change your attitude about them. Take your pick. That is, stop seeing people who upset you, hire a credit counselor to dig yourself out of debt or look at your current work situation as merely a stepping stone to bigger and better things. Booze can no longer be your crutch.

Think about the people and situations that get on your nerves and drive you to drink. Describe them and how you'll deal with them without alcohol.

Notes

_____

_____

_____

_____

_____

_____

_____

_____

_____

_____

_____

_____

_____

_____

_____

_____

_____

_____

_____

_____

WATCH YOUR DRINKING DVD

It's time to take a look at yourself when you're under the influence. Screen the DVD your pal made of you when you were drinking, as previously suggested. Congratulations if you kept your head and stayed within your limit! If you didn't, see how wild, crazy, mean or sleepy you get when you drink too much.

Don't beat yourself up over this DVD. That's not the point of this exercise. Rather, use it for future reference and review it when you're facing a drinking challenge. It might deter you from going all out and getting drunk again.

How do you behave when you've had one too many? Write about it.

BEAT BINGE DRINKING

I f you get drunk most every time you drink, binge drinking is your vice. It's that all-or-nothing-at-all mindset that dictates once you start drinking you can't stop. You go all out - no matter what.

Here are a few tips to beat binge drinking. First, ask yourself where you picked up this adolescent form of problem drinking. Did you learn it from high school or college buddies? From parents? Remind yourself those days are over and you're no longer a rebellious teenager.

Second, if circumstances in your life are so intolerable that you binge to blot them out, you've got to address them. Serious self-examination and healthy, appropriate ways to deal with the issues behind your bingeing will help. Think about it. Then put your thoughts into actions.

More strategies to beat binge drinking? Pre-plan, pre-plan, pre-plan! Know how long you'll drink, how many drinks you'll have, watch the clock and eat while you drink. And talk to yourself. Give yourself a passionate payoff pep talk full of positives, like how great you'll feel in

Notes

the morning and how you won't have to worry about your reputation, when you don't binge and stick to your limit. Others have whipped binge drinking and you can too - with commitment, motivation, pre-planning and action.

Record your payoff pep talk and drinking plan for the next time you're in the mood to binge. Then follow through with them when needed.

Moderate Drinking Made Easy Workbook

HALT HABITUAL DRINKING

Are you in a drinking rut? Do you start drinking at about the same time, the same place and have the same number of drinks? If nothing stands between you and your happy hour, you're a slave to habitual drinking.

Having a few alcohol-free days every week is one way to break the routine. Pre-plan all of your soft drinks, snacks and activities for the times you usually drink alcohol and you'll forget about that vodka tonic in no time. Alter how you drink on drinking days too. If you start at five, start at six instead. Begin with a snack and soda. Alternate with non-alcoholic drinks. Stop at eight, instead of nine. Anything to break the old pattern.

And don't forget your passionate payoff pep talk! The one where you tell yourself how happy and free you'll feel when you no longer have an alcohol habit. Don't drink a couple of days a week, mix up your drinking style on drinking days and give yourself a motivating payoff pep talk and you'll halt habitual drinking.

List the days you'll abstain and your plans for the days you'll drink.

STOP STRESS DRINKING

I t's no wonder you might turn to alcohol to relieve stress. It's legal, convenient, requires no energy and you're high within minutes.

Better stress-reducing activities may require a little more effort on your part. Instead of drinking, take a brisk walk. Or play the piano. Or take a swim. Or listen to a relaxation tape. Or have safe sex. Or practice yoga. Or meditate. Or take a bubble bath. Or take a cat nap. What relaxes you without alcohol? Next time stress is getting you down, commit yourself to a healthier way of dealing with it, instead of having a glass of wine.

And don't forget to give yourself a stirring payoff pep talk! Reminding you of how sweet your life will be when you don't have to rely on booze to relax.

Jot down ten stress-reducing activities you enjoy. Then do them, instead of having a cocktail.

Moderate Drinking Made Easy Workbook

EXTINGUISH
EMOTIONAL DRINKING

Do you drink when you're happy, sad or mad? You could be an emotional or mood drinker - using alcohol to accent good feelings and numb bad ones.

Next time you find yourself reaching for the bottle when you're happy, step back and ask yourself what you're doing. Couldn't you enjoy this moment without liquor? Is it really necessary to have a couple of cocktails to enhance your good mood? It's not! Then celebrate with a spa treatment or a nice dinner out instead.

If you drink to numb sad or mad feelings, rethink your reaction. Downing liquor to soothe negative emotions is not what a healthy person does. A sensible drinker exercises to feel better. Or calls a friend to get troubles off their chest. Or pops a comedy into the DVD player. They don't drown their sorrows in alcohol.

And don't forget your motivating payoff pep talk. Just think how great you'll feel when you no longer need to medicate your emotions with booze.

Brainstorm and record how you'll deal with your mood the next time you're facing emotional drinking.

Notes

REJECT REFLEXIVE DRINKING

Reflexive drinking is automatic drinking in response to feelings, moods, people, places, events or situations. Having a cocktail first thing when you get home from work. Having a beer when you wash your car. Pouring a glass of wine with lunch. Getting smashed with your best friend. Overdoing it at your favorite restaurant. Drinkers who engage in reflexive drinking don't think before they drink. It's a knee-jerk reaction and they just start guzzling.

Are you a reflexive drinker? If you are, talk yourself out of it, remember your commitment to moderate drinking, motivate yourself with a passionate payoff pep talk and devise and follow through with a drinking plan to prevent it. It's not rocket science.

Describe the feelings, moods, people, places, events or situations that trigger your reflexive drinking. Then write about how you'll reject it.

MANAGE MINDLESS DRINKING

Drinking while you're watching TV. Drinking while you're doing laundry. Drinking while you're watering the lawn. Drinking for no good reason is mindless drinking.

Mindless drinking may improve your mood when you're just passing time or doing boring chores, but it's inappropriate drinking. And it adds to your alcohol consumption. Appropriate drinking, on the other hand, involves eating, partying with people you like or raising your glass to celebrate.

Save drinks for the fun, special times of your life, not the mundane stuff. When you're compelled to start drinking for no good reason, reflect on appropriate and inappropriate drinking. Then think about the toll alcohol takes on your body and where you'll be ten years from now if you continue to drink mindlessly. Maybe you'll get the message.

Record the last time you engaged in mindless drinking. Then write about why you want to put an end to it.

Notes

_____

_____

_____

_____

_____

_____

_____

_____

_____

_____

_____

_____

_____

_____

_____

_____

_____

_____

GET OFF THE STARVING,
BINGEING MERRY-GO-ROUND

D o you starve yourself all day so you can drink all night? That's what some people do to keep the pounds off. And it's the sign of a problem drinker.

Put an end to this madness - not eating nutritious food in favor of drinking empty alcohol calories. Get off the starving, bingeing merry-go-round. Your health, well-being and problem drinking are all at stake.

When was the last time you fasted in favor of drinking? Write about it and how you'll do things differently in the future.

DON'T OVERDO DRINKING DAYS

Abstaining a couple of days a week has its merits. It interrupts your old problem drinking routine and starts you thinking about other ways to cope instead of drinking.

Yes, having several alcohol-free days a week is a great step in the right direction. But watch it. Be careful not to overdo it on your drinking days. You know, thinking you deserve extra drinks because you were so good for sticking to your abstinent days. Drinking thinking like that will get you back to square one in no time.

What's your mindset after you've successfully abstained for one, two or three days? Describe it.

Notes

_____

_____

_____

_____

_____

_____

_____

_____

_____

_____

_____

_____

_____

_____

_____

_____

_____

_____

A MINI-DRINK MAY
BE THE WAY TO GO

You're thrilled. You've been staying within your daily and weekly drink limits for weeks and now you're ready to take the next big step - cutting down a little more. Do it painlessly and effortlessly by only pouring a half drink for your last drink of the day, instead of a whole one.

Just a half glass of wine, a half bottle of beer or a half shot of liquor with lots of mixer, instead of a whole second or third cocktail, and you'll cut down even more. Wasn't that easy?

Are you ready to drink less? Are you ready for mini-drinks? Make your argument for mini- drinks in the space.

Notes

Moderate Drinking Made Easy Workbook

TRY SUBLIMINAL SUGGESTIONS

You've recorded your payoff pep talk - all the reasons why you want to switch to moderate drinking - on a CD or audio cassette. Now, every night, listen to it when you go to bed. Allow yourself to doze off as you're listening - you're not required to be conscious or fully awake to derive the benefits from it.

Perhaps some of the very good reasons to drink moderately in your payoff pep talk will seep into your subconscious and improve your conscious drinking behavior. You'll never know until you try it!

Listen to your payoff pep talk at bedtime for one month. Does it help? Record your thoughts.

Notes

_____

_____

_____

_____

_____

_____

_____

_____

_____

_____

_____

_____

_____

_____

_____

_____

_____

_____

COULD HYPNOSIS WORK?

If stress, depression, anxiety or anger drives you to drink, pick up a hypnosis CD that deals with whatever is bothering you. Or book an appointment with a real, live hypnotist who specializes in what you're concerned about. Many people swear by hypnosis to change attitudes and behaviors. What have you got to lose? A bad attitude and a drinking problem!

In the meantime, brainstorm and list all the different ways you can relieve the feelings that drive you to drink.

COULD HERBS BE HELPFUL?

ome all-natural herbs have been shown to take the edge off of alcohol craving. A word to the wise though. If you think just popping a pill or taking an herb will put an end to your drinking desire, you're wrong. The only long-term solution to reducing alcohol craving is to address the issues behind it and cultivate sensible drinking skills and attitudes. An herb may help you stick to your healthy drinking plan, but it's not the answer to any drinking problem.

Research herbs that may reduce alcohol craving. Then write about them - their effects and side effects.

Notes

_____
_____
_____
_____
_____
_____
_____
_____
_____
_____
_____
_____
_____
_____
_____
_____
_____
_____

PERHAPS SUPPLEMENTS WOULD BE USEFUL

An amino acid is also thought to reduce alcohol craving. Again, taking a supplement will not eliminate drinking desire or a drinking problem. Modifying your actions and attitudes around liquor will.

Research and write about the effects and side effects of supplements that might step on your alcohol craving.

HOW ABOUT THERAPY CDS?

Dealing with stress, depression, anger and anxiety - feelings that may trigger alcohol craving - with cognitive-behavioral or rational-emotive therapy CDs may also be helpful. You could address the underlying issues behind your problem drinking and you might drink less.

If you go the CD route, jot down the effects they have on you and your drinking.

Notes

_____

_____

_____

_____

_____

_____

_____

_____

_____

_____

_____

_____

_____

_____

_____

_____

_____

ASKING FOR HELP IS OK

If you're having a hard time sticking to moderate drinking guidelines, talk to a trusted friend, relative or clergyman about changing your drinking habits and drinking less. They might keep you focused and on track - especially when you're facing a craving or a dangerous drinking situation. A friend in need is a friend indeed.

Who can you call in a time of need? List them and their telephone numbers. Then when you're feeling challenged, call them.

CONSIDER A SUPPORT GROUP

If talking to family and friends about your drinking problem is out of the question, how about getting together with other people who are struggling with the same problem? A support group could be several friends dealing with the same issue. It could be a planned meeting of people wanting to moderate their drinking habits and swapping tips and ideas on how to do it. Or it could be an online chat room where drinkers wanting to cut down exchange stories and offer support.

Research shows support groups work for people who want to change their ways. Getting your secrets, questions and concerns about booze off your chest can set you free. Free to make the transition to healthier drinking.

How can you connect with other problem drinkers who want to reduce their alcohol consumption? Research your resources and list them.

Notes

_____

_____

_____

_____

_____

_____

_____

_____

_____

_____

_____

_____

_____

_____

_____

_____

_____

_____

_____

HAVE A GOOD CRY

Notes

_____

_____

_____

_____

_____

_____

_____

_____

_____

_____

_____

_____

_____

_____

_____

_____

_____

_____

I f you've had a bad day, you're up to your neck in problems and you're fighting a fierce drinking desire, let it all out and have a good cry. Release all that tension and frustration. You'll feel cleansed and renewed. Your need to drink may fade. And you'll be ready to make a fresh start.

When was the last time you let it all out and had a good cry? Did you feel better? Did it reduce your alcohol craving? Describe your feelings.

Moderate Drinking Made Easy Workbook

MODERATE DRINKING PROGRAMS WORK

You might consider a moderate drinking program to keep you on the straight and narrow. Brief interventions, like a moderate drinking program, have been shown to help early-stage problem drinkers modify their drinking habits and reduce their alcohol consumption. If you would like a more structured approach offering the support you need to achieve your sensible drinking goal, check them out.

Which moderate drinking programs might work for you? Look into them, then list them.

Notes

_____

_____

_____

_____

_____

_____

_____

_____

_____

_____

_____

_____

_____

_____

_____

_____

_____

_____

_____

_____

YOUR DESIRE TO DRINK
WILL FADE OVER TIME

Great news! You won't have to suffer from alcohol craving for the rest of your life. How long it takes to fade depends a lot on your lifestyle and alcohol attitude adjustment. That is, how much energy you put into taking the focus off of liquor and into healthy living and relationships.

What attitude and lifestyle changes are reducing your desire to drink? Jot them down.

Moderate Drinking Made Easy Workbook

SPIRITUAL PRACTICE YES, DRINKING NO

U ntil now, perhaps drinking and getting lost in the euphoria of alcohol was your only spiritual practice. Ironically, spirits get in touch with your spirit.

But that was then and this is now. Cultivating a spiritual practice, that does not require alcohol, is another giant step to make liquor less important in your life - so it complements your existence, instead of being the center of it.

God, soul, divine self, essence of being. There are many different names for spirit and many ways to get in touch with it, other than drinking. Perhaps conventional religion would be the answer for you. Or new age religion, which teaches spirit dwells in each of us, would be. Maybe eastern spiritual practices, like Buddhism, yoga or meditation, would be more to your liking. Or music or art would be the pathway to your spiritual self. Maybe thrilling new experiences, like swimming with sharks or skiing the Alps, would tap into your soulful nature. Or giving

Notes

yourself to others would - like volunteering for a charity that is near and dear to your heart.

How can you get in touch with your spiritual side without liquor? Think about it, write down your options and pursue them.

HARMONIOUS LIVING
NURTURES MODERATE DRINKING

The happier, healthier and more balanced you are physically, psychologically, intellectually, spiritually and socially, the less inclined you'll be to turn to substances and activities - like alcohol, food or gambling - to improve your mood.

What aspects of your life need more nurturing? What aspects need less nurturing? Getting too much or too little physical activity? Getting too much or too little intellectual stimulation? Working too much or too little? Playing too much or too little? Are you starving spiritually or devoting too much time to spiritual pursuits? It's up to you to examine and equalize your life.

Jot down areas of your life you need to work on a little more or a little less. Then record specific plans on how to achieve your perfect balance. You might just drink less.

Notes

_____

_____

_____

_____

_____

_____

_____

_____

_____

_____

_____

_____

_____

_____

_____

_____

_____

_____

_____

_____

STOP OBSESSING ABOUT
WHAT YOU'RE GIVING UP

Unhappy about cutting down? Miserable just thinking about alcohol-free days? Those feelings won't last forever. In the meantime, think about your payoffs. Like no alcohol-related health problems. Improved relationships with mate, family, friends and colleagues. No legal or financial concerns because of liquor. Your fine reputation remains in tact and isn't tainted by alcohol. And you'll never worry about your drinking again - the ultimate payoff.

Stop obsessing about what you're giving up - more drinks. Instead, obsess about how good your life will be when you keep your drinking in check.

Write down all the ways your life will change for the better if you control alcohol and drink moderately.

ARE YOU THINKING OUTSIDE OF THE BOTTLE?

Are you enjoying more alcohol-free activities? It's a priority if you're committed to improving your drinking habits. There is life outside of the bottle.

But if you're still just sitting around, drinking and thinking about life without so much liquor, it's time to put that drink down, put your thoughts into action and take that hike, bake that cake, do those sit-ups, join that club, call that friend or go to that matinee . . .

What fun alcohol-free activities do you have planned for the next week? List them. Then fit them into your schedule and follow through!

Notes

_____

_____

_____

_____

_____

_____

_____

_____

_____

_____

_____

_____

_____

_____

_____

_____

_____

_____

Moderate Drinking Made Easy Workbook

ARE YOU BUILDING A REPERTOIRE OF SAFE DRINKING SKILLS?

What tips, skills, strategies and techniques are helping you stick to your drink limits? You're building a repertoire of safe drinking skills that will help you achieve and maintain moderate drinking for the rest of your life.

Jot down every tip, skill, strategy and technique that has enabled you to stay within your drink limit. Then keep practicing the ones that work for you!

ARE YOU BECOMING
A DRINKING DETECTIVE?

Have you been keeping your drinking diary? Recording how much you drink, how long you drink, the date, day, time, companions, circumstances and physiological and psychological factors that may drive you to drink?

Here's where the detective work comes in. Look at all of your entries. Can you pinpoint the variables that trigger your alcohol craving and overdrinking? Do you start drinking as soon as you're off work or just on the weekends? Do you do most of your drinking alone or with others? Do you drink more at home or when you're out? Do you drink to fight boredom, relieve stress, numb emotions or all three? What other factors may be pushing your drinking buttons?

Play Sherlock Holmes and figure out when, where and why you start drinking and drink too much at times. Then brainstorm different ways to handle these variables so they don't lead to a drinking response. Elementary my dear Watson, if you're going to switch to moderate drinking.

List all the variables that trigger your alcohol craving and overdrinking.

Notes

_____
_____
_____
_____
_____
_____
_____
_____
_____
_____
_____
_____
_____
_____
_____
_____
_____
_____
_____
_____
_____

ARE YOU IMPROVISING?

_____

_____

_____

_____

_____

_____

_____

_____

_____

_____

_____

_____

_____

_____

_____

_____

_____

_____

_____

_____

Y ou've got to go with the flow in any drinking situation. If you're caught off guard and find it difficult to stick to your plan, do your best to improvise so you can stay within your drink limit. Keep what works of the original plan and get creative with the rest. Add simple skills to get you through, like pacing yourself, delaying between drinks, alternating with non-alcoholic beverages and focusing on the company. Improvising a workable drinking plan on the spot? No problem!

When was the last time your drinking plan was thrown off? Describe it, what you did and what you should have done to stay on track.

Moderate Drinking Made Easy Workbook

THINK OF THE
POUNDS YOU'LL SHED

Want to lose a few pounds? Those extra pounds might be from the extra drinks you've been having.

Alcohol is fattening. It's full of empty, non-nutritious calories that don't do a thing for you, except increase your calorie intake. Just two beers, two glasses of wine or two mixed drinks contain between 200 and 400 calories! And if you have more than two drinks, you're adding even more calories which could lead to a serious weight gain.

The next time you're facing your moment of truth - when you're deciding if you should start or stop drinking - you can add losing a few pounds to your payoff pep talk. Then envision a happier, healthier, slimmer you, instead of an overweight, bloated one - the one you were when you were drinking too much.

How much weight have you lost since you've reduced your alcohol consumption? Record it and think about it the next time you want an extra drink.

Notes

_____

_____

_____

_____

_____

_____

_____

_____

_____

_____

_____

_____

_____

_____

_____

_____

_____

_____

WANT TO PLEASE YOUR MATE?

If alcohol comes between you and your significant other, imagine the delight you'll both take in you cutting down. No more nagging, no more fights about liquor, no more keeping an eye on how much you're drinking, no more babysitting you when you've had too much. How happy could you and your mate be if booze was no longer an issue?

Like it or not, if you have a history of alcohol-related problems spanning over a number of years, it might take a while for you to convince your loved one that liquor is no longer your priority. The only way you can accomplish this is to consistently behave like a moderate drinker - with no alcohol problems for months or even years.

Be patient with yourself and your mate during this process. They care about you. That's why they pester you about your drinking. Understand where they're coming from and you'll understand they need time to see you're a new, improved drinker.

Put yourself in your loved one's shoes and write about their feelings.

Moderate Drinking Made Easy Workbook

SMALL STEPS ADD UP TO MODERATE DRINKING

A significant improvement in your drinking behavior - like cutting your alcohol consumption in half - is the result of many small steps you take along the way. Practiced individually, simple skills like pacing yourself, eating while you drink and sipping, not gulping, won't lead to a noticeable reduction in your alcohol intake. But when all three skills are practiced together, you'll see a big difference.

What small steps are you taking? Jot them down.

Notes

_____

_____

_____

_____

_____

_____

_____

_____

_____

_____

_____

_____

_____

_____

_____

_____

_____

_____

LEAVE TOXIC
SHAME BEHIND

No more regrets about what you said or did in the past when you were high on alcohol. No more wasting your precious energy reliving unpleasant events fueled by liquor. No more wishing you could have changed things and daydreaming about what you could have done differently when you were under the influence.

All of us carry baggage from the past that eats away at our self-esteem. Unfortunately, holding on to the shame of past events will make your transition to moderate drinking more difficult. So instead of continuing to beat yourself up over past mistakes, learn from them and move on. You've grown and you're making a real effort to change.

Record alcohol-related events in your past that you're ashamed of. Get them off your chest, then focus on your bright future.

LOVE YOURSELF

The more you like yourself, the less you'll engage in destructive behavior. So taking good care of yourself, physically and psychologically, are prerequisites to improving your drinking behavior. Putting yourself first automatically puts booze last.

How can you take even better care of yourself so you'll succeed at moderate drinking? List the ways.

LIVE FREE

I magine you're no longer a slave to alcohol, it's no longer a monkey on your back and it's no longer a deep, dark, shameful secret. You're living life free from alcohol abuse!

How will you feel when you don't have problem drinking to worry about? Describe your feelings.

Moderate Drinking Made Easy Workbook

SO MANY POSITIVE CHANGES, SO LITTLE TIME

Changing from a problem drinker to a moderate drinker will transform your life in so many different ways. Physically, psychologically, emotionally, intellectually, spiritually and socially.

What positive changes can you look forward to when you perfect the art of moderate drinking? Write about them.

Notes

_____

_____

_____

_____

_____

_____

_____

_____

_____

_____

_____

_____

_____

_____

_____

_____

_____

_____

_____

_____

FACE THE FEAR OF FAILURE AND DEFEAT IT

Afraid you can't make the moderate drinking grade? Afraid you'll fail and revert back to your old ways? Face those fears head on. Acknowledge them. They're normal when you're challenging deeply ingrained behaviors.

How do you defeat your fears? By being firmly committed, highly motivated, well-prepared with a safe drinking plan and following through with it!

Reflect on the fear of not meeting your sensible drinking goal. Write about it. Then put it behind you.

SAY HELLO TO A BRAND
NEW CHAPTER IN YOUR LIFE

You can turn over a new leaf as far as your drinking goes. You can turn troubled relationships and work, money and legal problems around when you commit to moderate drinking. This healthy new chapter in your life may take some time to write and may need editing here and there, but it could happen.

How does the new sensible drinking chapter in your life read? Describe it.

Notes

_____

_____

_____

_____

_____

_____

_____

_____

_____

_____

_____

_____

_____

_____

_____

_____

_____

_____

_____

CHART YOUR MODERATE DRINKING JOURNEY

S witching from problem drinking to moderate drinking is a journey with ups and downs. Take your time, be patient with yourself and you'll arrive safely at your destination.

Chart your moderate drinking journey. First, record the date and your daily and weekly drink totals before you started your trip. Then record the date and your daily and weekly drink totals when you've reduced your alcohol consumption by one-quarter. Do the same when you've cut your drinking in half and when your intake is down by three-quarters. Then remove this page and frame it. Keep it as a reminder.

Congratulations! You made your moderate drinking goal!

Moderate Drinking Made Easy Workbook

Chapter Five:

How Are You Doing?

H ave you reduced your alcohol craving and consumption and put alcohol in perspective? Look at your daily and weekly drink totals. Have you noticed a gradual decrease in the number of drinks you're having? One or two per drinking occasion, instead of four or five, like you use to have? Are you having fewer overdrinking episodes? Fewer hangovers? All factors you must consider to see if you've made the switch to moderate drinking.

Have your family, friends and colleagues noticed a difference in you and your drinking? Have they observed you cutting down and commented on it? No more alcohol-related problems at home or work because you're drinking less? More factors you should consider when evaluating your progress.

You're the judge if moderate drinking is working for you. Be honest with yourself. If you have a hard time sticking to your drink limits, you go overboard on a regular basis and you spend a lot of time thinking about drinking, drinking or recovering from it, moderate drinking is not working for you.

Lying to yourself about your drinking problem will only prolong it. Instead of suffering from years of alcohol abuse and its consequences, stand up, be an adult, take responsibility and stop drinking.

Consider Other Alternatives

If you think getting by on less booze is impossible or quitting might be easier, simply go on the wagon. Alcoholics Anonymous - AA - is still the most popular abstinence approach around. It was founded in 1935 by a New York stockbroker and an Ohio surgeon, both alcoholics, who wanted to help others achieve and maintain sobriety. Members stay away from alcohol by following a Twelve Step program, believing in a higher power and sharing their experiences at free AA meetings.

The Secular Organization for Sobriety - SOS - is another popular abstinence approach. It's also free and has meetings where members offer support to achieve and maintain sobriety. Unlike AA, SOS emphasizes self-empowerment - encouraging personal responsibility and crediting the individual for stopping drinking on their own. It does not follow the Twelve Step program or require a belief in a higher power, but urges a scientific approach to understanding alcoholism.

You can find AA or SOS meetings in your area by looking in the yellow pages under "Alcoholism Information and Treatment" or logging on to www.aa.org or www.secularsobriety.org.

If AA or SOS don't appeal to you, there are many other abstinence programs available. Again, dig in, do your homework and decide which one would work for you, then follow through.

About the Author
Donna J. Cornett, M.A.

Donna J. Cornett is the founder and director of Drink/Link Moderate Drinking Programs and Products. She holds an M.A. and California College Teaching Credential in psychology and believes offering drinkers a moderate drinking goal, instead of life-long abstinence, is the key to motivating them to seek early treatment and to preventing alcohol abuse.

Cornett was in her thirties when she realized she was drinking too much and would be facing a serious drinking problem if she did not address it. At that time, her only options were abstinence, AA or to keep drinking. There was no middle-of-the-road alcohol education program teaching drinkers sensible drinking habits and attitudes so they could avoid alcohol abuse. And like many drinkers, she did not believe her drinking was serious enough to stop altogether or in the concept of a higher power to help her cut down.

Consequently, Cornett developed Drink/Link in 1988 - long before any other moderate drinking programs were available in the United States. This commonsense program teaches drinkers to modify their drinking habits, reduce their alcohol craving and consumption and prevent alcoholism.

Donna J. Cornett is also the author of *7 Weeks to Safe Social Drinking: How to Effectively Moderate Your Alcohol Intake* and *Moderate Drinking - Naturally! Herbs and Vitamins to Control Your Drinking*. She has been featured or consulted for articles in Time Magazine, the New York Post, ABCNews.com, Esquire, Scripps Howard News Service and professional publications. Her latest achievement is offering drinkers everywhere the first affordable, over-the-counter alcohol abuse prevention program - The Sensible Drinking System.

To contact Donna Cornett, email her at info@drinklinkmoderation.com, call her at 707-539-5465 or write her at P.O. Box 5441, Santa Rosa, California, 95402, USA.

About Drink/Link™

Moderate Drinking Programs and Products

Drink/Link Moderate Drinking Programs and Products was established in 1988 and has helped thousands of drinkers worldwide to modify drinking habits and attitudes, reduce alcohol craving and consumption and prevent alcoholism. Drink/Link was the first moderate drinking program in the United States and the first registered with both the California Department of Drug and Alcohol Programs and the United States Department of Health and Human Services.

All Drink/Link Programs are based on commonsense safe drinking guidelines and clinically-proven behavioral, cognitive, motivational and lifestyle strategies and techniques to stay within those guidelines. The most intensive programs, which include professional counseling, are the Email Counseling Program and the Telephone Counseling Program. The Self-Study Program and the Sensible Drinking System are self-help programs you complete on your own at home.

Drink/Link also offers a line of moderate drinking products. Contact Drink/Link directly at www.drinklinkmoderation.com to view the product catalog.

Drink/Link™
Moderate Drinking Programs and Products
P.O. Box 5441
Santa Rosa, California USA 95402
Local: 707-539-5465 Toll-Free: 888-773-7465
Fax: 707-537-1010
Email: info@drinklinkmoderation.com
www.drinklinkmoderation.com

Drink/Link™

Moderate Drinking Programs and Products

ORDER FORM

<u>Order Your Own Copies of</u>

7 Weeks to Safe Social Drinking:
How to Effectively Moderate Your Alcohol Intake
By Donna J. Cornett

Moderate Drinking - Naturally!
Herbs and Vitamins to Control Your Drinking
By Donna J. Cornett

PLEASE CIRCLE BOOKS OF CHOICE

7 Weeks to Safe Social Drinking $18.95

Moderate Drinking - Naturally! $18.95

Number of books:	Cost of books:
Shipping & Handling: (U.S. $4.95 for the first book. Outside U.S. $6.95 for the first and $4.95 for each additional book. Shipped U.S. Mail.)	
Subtotal:	
State Tax: (California residents please add tax)	
Final Total:	
Payment Enclosed	Please charge to my credit card(Visa, MasterCard, American Express)

Account # _____

Expiration Date: _____

Signature: _____

PLEASE SEND TO:

Name:	
Institution:	
Address:	
City:	State/Zip:
Country:	Telephone:
Email:	

Drink/Link™
Moderate Drinking Programs and Products
P.O. Box 5441
Santa Rosa, California USA 95402
Local: 707-539-5465 Toll-Free: 888-773-7465
Fax: 707-537-1010
Email: info@drinklinkmoderation.com
www.drinklinkmoderation.com

Drink/Link™

Moderate Drinking Programs and Products

ORDER FORM

FOR A COMPLETE LISTING OF PROGRAMS AND PRODUCTS

LOGON TO:

www.drinklinkmoderation.com

Local: 707- 539-5465

Toll-Free: 888-773-7465

The Drink/Link Self-Study Program - $195.00

This program includes a 50-minute telephone consultation with Donna Cornett personally - examining your current drinking habits and offering you tips to drink less tailored to your lifestyle. Also included is the workbook, *7 Weeks to Safe Social Drinking*, the CD, "Control Your Drinking - Now!", a Drinking Diary, Drink Graph, Nutritional Supplements and Step-by-Step Instructions so you can successfully complete the program on your own at home.

The Sensible Drinking System - $65.00

This over-the-counter program offers the basics - the workbook, *7 Weeks to Safe Social Drinking*, the CD, "Control Your Drinking - Now!", a Drinking Diary, Drink Graph and Step-by-Step Instructions so you can successfully complete the program on your own at home.

PLEASE CIRCLE THE PROGRAM OF CHOICE

| The Drink/Link Self-Study Program | $195.00 |
| The Drink/Link Sensible Drinking System | $65.00 |

Number of programs:	Cost of programs:
Shipping & Handling: (U.S. $10.00 for the first program. Outside U.S. $15.00 for the first and $10.00 for each additional program. Shipped U.S. Mail.)	
Subtotal:	
State Tax: (California residents please add tax)	
Final Total:	
Payment Enclosed	Please charge to my credit card(Visa, MasterCard, American Express)
Account #	
Expiration Date:	
Signature:	

PLEASE SEND TO:

Name:	
Institution:	
Address:	
City:	State/Zip:
Country:	Telephone:
Email:	

Drink/Link™
Moderate Drinking Programs and Products
P.O. Box 5441
Santa Rosa, California USA 95402
Local: 707-539-5465 Toll-Free: 888-773-7465
Fax: 707-537-1010
Email: info@drinklinkmoderation.com
www.drinklinkmoderation.com

17070060R00130

Printed in Great Britain
by Amazon